HEINEMANN MATHEMATICS 3

Teacher's Notes

HEINEMANN MATHEMATICS 3

Teacher's Notes

For **Level 2** and towards **Level 3** of the National
Curriculum (England and Wales, and Northern Ireland)
and towards **Level B** of Mathematics 5–14 (Scotland).

Heinemann Educational,
a division of Heinemann Educational Books Ltd,
Halley Court, Jordan Hill, Oxford OX2 8EJ

OXFORD LONDON EDINBURGH
MADRID ATHENS BOLOGNA PARIS
MELBOURNE SYDNEY AUCKLAND SINGAPORE TOKYO
IBADAN NAIROBI HARARE GABORONE
PORTSMOUTH NH (USA)

Writing team
Archie MacCallum
John Thayers
John T Blair
Aileen Duncan
Myra A Pearson
David Thomson
Ian K Clark
John Mackinlay
David McInnes
Catherine D J Preston
William W R Tait

Designed by Miller, Craig & Cocking
Produced by Gecko Limited, Bicester, Oxon

Printed in the UK by Scotprint Ltd, Edinburgh.

ISBN 0 435 02095 1

Preface

Heinemann Mathematics is a new course which offers continuous development from nursery through the infant and junior stages to secondary level and aims to help children to apply mathematics in a variety of situations. It has been created by the Scottish Primary Mathematics Group, augmented by experienced nursery, primary and secondary teachers. The new material draws on feedback from practising teachers and experience gained from years of classroom use of the original SPMG course, 'Primary Mathematics – A development through activity'.

A Practical Approach

The course is based on the belief that mathematics is best learned through practical activities, discussion and teaching by the teacher. The use of materials, diagrams, and pictures to help pupils acquire concepts and understand techniques is encouraged throughout the Heinemann Mathematics course.

Problem Solving and Investigation

There is an emphasis on problem solving and investigative work. Pupils are encouraged to use their mathematics to solve practical, mathematical and real-life problems. Suggestions are given for introducing and developing some topics in an investigative way.

Contexts

Mathematics is presented in context wherever possible so that it can be seen to relate to the world outside the classroom and the world of the child's imagination. Such contexts are more likely to stimulate an interest in mathematics and encourage positive attitudes.

Calculation

Heinemann Mathematics encourages mental methods of calculation as well as the development of paper and pencil techniques and also the use of calculators for certain computations. Calculators are also used at appropriate points to introduce concepts and to solve problems.

Approach to Learning and Teaching

The approach adopted in Heinemann Mathematics is in tune with the guidelines provided by the National Curriculum (England and Wales), Mathematics 5–14 (Scotland) and the Northern Ireland Curriculum. The course has been designed to provide teachers with resources and a structure to meet the requirements of each curriculum. Assessment material linked to attainment targets is included.

Teachers will wish to select from the materials provided as part of a broader strategy of teaching, where resources are matched to the needs and abilities of individuals. A variety of formats such as workbooks, cards, textbooks and photocopiable masters is employed so that the course materials can be used flexibly in ways which suit particular teachers and children.

Contents

Introduction

Heinemann Mathematics 3 is intended for use with children
- finishing Level 2 and starting Level 3 of the National Curriculum (England and Wales, and Northern Ireland)
- starting Level B of Mathematics 5–14 (Scotland)

STRUCTURE OF THE RESOURCES

The Heinemann Mathematics 3 materials consist of
- Teacher's Notes
- Workbooks
- Textbook
- Answer Book
- Assessment and Resources Pack

The Teacher's Notes suggest practical activities for introducing mathematical concepts and techniques. Written work for children is then provided in the workbooks, which in turn refer to specific Textbook pages. The use of a Textbook ensures that the children are given further opportunities to record their own work.

The Teacher's Notes also contain suggestions for further consolidation and additional activities. Assessment material related to the workbooks and Textbook is included in the Assessment and Resources Pack.

Workbooks

There are three workbooks. Workbooks 1 and 2, together with the associated Textbook pages, contain a sequence of work in Number, including money. The other workbook, with its associated Textbook pages, contains separate sections on topics in Measure, Shape and Handling data. The list below indicates the main sections within each workbook and in its associated Textbook pages.

Workbook 1 Number
■ Addition and subtraction facts for 14 to 20
■ Place value to 100 Approximation Addition of tens and units, including money
■ Subtraction of tens and units, including money

Workbook 2 Number
■ Multiplication (concept; 2, 3, 4, 5 and 10 times tables; money, including the £1 coin)
■ Division (concept of sharing; dividing by 2, 3, 4 and 5)
■ Fractions (notation for $\frac{1}{2}$, $\frac{1}{4}$, $\frac{3}{4}$; finding $\frac{1}{2}$ or $\frac{1}{4}$ of a set of objects)
■ Division (concept of grouping; dividing by 2, 3, 4 and 5)

Measure, Shape and Handling data Workbook
■ Time
■ Length
■ Area
■ Volume
■ Weight
■ Measure
■ 3D shape
■ Tiling
■ Right angles
■ Symmetry
■ Handling data

Charts giving fuller details of the mathematical content of Heinemann Mathematics 3 are shown on Pages 8 and 10.

Workbooks 1 and 2 should be used more or less in order, to provide a sequence of work in number and money.

Sections from the Measure, Shape and Handling data Workbook should be interspersed with the number sections from Workbooks 1 and 2 to give a balanced coverage of the various aspects of mathematics. The order in which the sections from the Measure, Shape and Handling data Workbook are used is flexible, to a considerable extent, and at the teacher's discretion. The end of each section of work in this workbook is indicated by the instruction

> **Ask your teacher what to do next.**

Some of the pages in the workbooks contain references to Textbook pages where the work of particular sections is continued. For example,

> **Go to Textbook page 31**

Textbook

As indicated above, the Textbook contains pages of work associated with some of the sections in the three workbooks. Such pages require the children to copy and complete work thus giving practice in recording without the support provided by the fill-in format of the workbooks. At times there are references back to a workbook page from the Textbook. For example, the following reference at the foot of Textbook Page 39 directs the children to continue their work on symmetry in the workbook:

> **Go back to Measure, Shape and Handling data Workbook, page 30, question 1**

Some sections of work finish on a Textbook page. This is usually indicated by

> **Ask your teacher what to do next.**

The Textbook also contains pages labelled 'Other activity'. Many of these pages contain activities of an investigative, problem solving, extension or practical nature.

Special Features

'Other activity' pages

These pages are identified in the Textbook by a 'purple' teacher's heading (see Textbook Page i) and in the Teacher's Notes by a tint of red. They are intended to give further opportunities for children to apply the mathematics they have been learning or to extend their experience. A small number of pages of this type is associated with each workbook. (See the record of work grid on the back of each workbook.)

These pages may be used in any order as long as the related concepts have been introduced. The teaching notes for the pages give advice about this. The teacher should choose when one of these activities is used, and the pupils for whom it is appropriate.

Problem solving, Investigation, Extension

Throughout the workbooks and Textbook, 'flags' have been included to indicate that a page or a question contains a particular kind of work. This is also indicated in the Overview for each section of work, in the Teacher's Notes.

Problem solving	indicates work of a non-routine nature which will require mathematical thinking if the children are to find a solution to the problem. Pages which contain problem solving activities are indicated in the record of work grids on the last page of each workbook.
Investigation	involves the children in finding out about a mathematical situation for themselves.
Extension	indicates either an extension to the range of a mathematical topic which many pupils may use, or more difficult examples suited to more able pupils.

Calculators is used to indicate that the use of a calculator may be appropriate. Calculators are used throughout to introduce concepts, to extend the work of topics and to solve problems.

Recording When using the Textbook it is assumed that the children will use an exercise book or jotter, or some other method of recording work. The symbol is used in the workbooks to indicate the few questions which should be answered in an exercise book.

Structured apparatus
Use tens and units if you wish

is used to indicate that tens and units blocks should be available for the children to use. Dienes or Tillich base 10 material would be suitable for this purpose.

Contexts

The activities in the workbooks and Textbook are set in context wherever possible. For example, the first half of Workbook 1, dealing with addition and subtraction facts for totals 14 to 20, relates to a Mystery Tour when the children visit Sun Town Funpark, Bug World, the Planetarium, etc. Sometimes the context appears as a scenario or a game on one or two pages to lend interest and realism to a particular activity.

Further details of these contexts are given in the section 'Using the Course' on Page 12.

Teacher's Notes

The Teacher's Notes are the central element of the course. They make suggestions about teaching methods and mathematical content. They also indicate how the workbooks, Textbook and Assessment and Resources Pack can be used to give a well-balanced course covering the attainment targets of the curriculum followed by your school.

For each workbook the Teacher's Notes contains a general description of all of the sections in that workbook and its associated Textbook pages. For each section there is an Overview which describes the purpose and content of the workbook, Textbook and Teacher's Notes pages for that section. 'Key words and phrases' and 'Resources' for the section are also listed.

Summary of the aims and mathematical content of each workbook together with its associated Textbook pages and teaching notes.

Workbook pages which contain extension, problem solving or investigative activities are highlighted.

List of materials useful for workbook and Textbook pages and introductory teaching activities.

Specific references to appropriate items from the Assessment and Resources Pack.

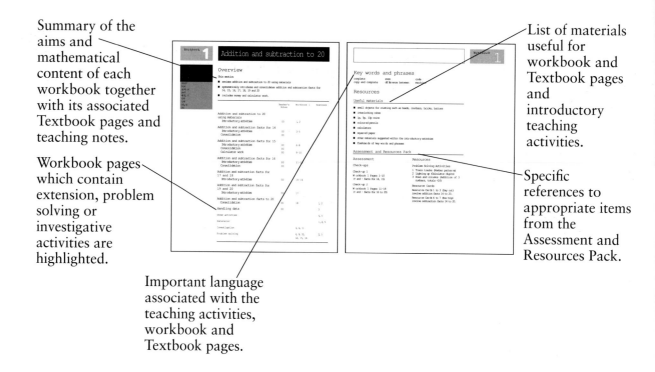

Important language associated with the teaching activities, workbook and Textbook pages.

These pages are followed by the teaching notes which give

- a variety of practical activities from which the teacher can *select* to introduce each new section of the work
- brief notes about groups of workbook or Textbook pages which follow up each new topic
- specific suggestions for oral work and consolidation where appropriate
- additional activities to provide further practice and extension
- advice about introducing the extended contexts which underlie some of the workbook and Textbook pages
- more extended notes about some of the 'Other activity' pages which appear in the Textbook
- references to attainment targets

Answer Book

The Answer Book contains photo reductions of the workbook pages with the answers inserted. There are also lists of answers for each Textbook page.

Assessment and Resources Pack

The Pack contains a variety of assessment and resource material, including photocopiable record sheets. The teacher should select materials from the Pack to suit the needs of particular children.

Assessment

There are two types of assessment in the pack: Check-ups and Assessment in Context. The Problem Solving Activities booklet outlined on Page 5 could also be used for assessment purposes.

Check-ups

This booklet contains twenty-two check-up sheets altogether. Seven relate to topics in Workbook 1, seven to Workbook 2 and the remaining eight to the Measure, Shape and Handling data Workbook. Each check-up is provided as a black and white A4 photocopiable sheet of short questions for direct use with the children. The booklet also gives answers and advice to teachers about the use of the material. Each check-up relates to one or two specific topics and the questions are referenced to attainment targets.

Assessment in Context

There are five assessment contexts, each consisting of 14 or 15 questions related to the same theme and covering a range of attainment targets. The number and money questions in the first two tests are linked to Workbook 1, in the next two tests to Workbook 2, and in the last test they relate to both Workbooks 1 and 2. Each test also covers a selection of work from the Measure, Shape and Handling data Workbook.

A booklet for teachers provides for each context, advice, answers and a teacher's script which is intended to be read to the children as they attempt the test.

Resources

Problem Solving Activities

This booklet contains twenty-five activities in the form of photocopiable sheets for the children. These are intended to supplement the problem solving and investigative activities in the workbooks and Textbook. They could also be used for assessment purposes. The booklet gives answers and advice to teachers.

Resource Cards

The resource cards contain games, self-correcting activities and teaching aids linked to the activities in the Teacher's Notes, workbooks and Textbook. A set of notes for teachers gives details about preparing and using the cards.

Photocopiable cards also provide simple checklists to indicate curriculum coverage.

References to the Curriculum

Detailed references to attainment targets for the National Curriculum (England and Wales) and Mathematics 5–14 (Scotland) are included in the Teacher's Notes in the Overview to each section of work and in the Assessment and Resources Pack. These references are provided as an aid to planning and recording. It is not envisaged that teaching should follow targets in a slavish way.

References to the National Curriculum (England and Wales)

The Teacher's Notes contain detailed references to the statements of attainment within the five attainment targets. The referencing shows attainment target, level, and statement of attainment.
For example,

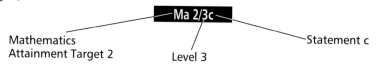

Ma 2/3c

Mathematics
Attainment Target 2

Level 3

Statement c

References to Mathematics 5–14 (Scotland)

In the Guidelines, the strands within each attainment outcome are not numbered or lettered. We have therefore devised a system of referencing using a code based on the initial letter(s) of each strand. The coding is as follows:

Attainment Outcome	Strand	Code
PROBLEM SOLVING and ENQUIRY		PSE
INFORMATION HANDLING	Collect	C
	Organise	O
	Display	D
	Interpret	I
NUMBER, MONEY and MEASUREMENT	Range and Type of Numbers	RTN
	Money	M
	Add and Subtract	AS
	Multiply and Divide	MD
	Round Numbers	RN
	Fractions, Percentages and Ratio	FPR
	Patterns and Sequences	PS
	Functions and Equations	FE
	Measure and Estimate	ME
	Time	T
	Perimeter, Formulae and Scales	PFS
SHAPE, POSITION and MOVEMENT	Range of Shapes	RS
	Position and Movement	PM
	Symmetry	S
	Angle	A

Each reference then consists of the *strand* code followed by the appropriate *level* and (for 'Overview' references) the *target*. For example,

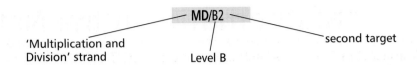

References to the Common Curriculum of Northern Ireland

At the time of producing these Teacher's Notes, we still await publication of the Common Curriculum. Full references to the statements of attainment for Northern Ireland will be included at a future reprint of the Teacher's Notes.

DEVELOPMENT CHARTS

The following Development Charts outline the mathematical content of Heinemann Mathematics 2 and 3.

One of the charts relates to Mathematics in the National Curriculum (England and Wales) while the other relates to Mathematics 5–14 (Scotland). A chart for the Common Curriculum of Northern Ireland will be supplied when further details are available.

Mathematics in the Nation

	Using and applying mathematics	Number		
		Knowledge and use of numbers	**Estimation and approximation**	**Measures**
HEINEMANN MATHEMATICS 2	Practical tasks, mathematical and real-life problems and investigations occur throughout	Subtraction facts – 7 to 10 Linking addition and subtraction facts within 10 Numbers to 20; Place value to 20 Using a calculator Numbers to 100; Place value to 99 (with material) Addition and subtraction facts to 13 Money to 50p (1p, 2p, 5p, 10p, 20p coins) Change from 5p and 10p Identifying halves and quarters		Using non-standard units – length, area, capacity, weight Commonly used units Telling the time – o'clock and h. past using analogue and digital displays Days of the week; months of th year
HEINEMANN MATHEMATICS 3	Practical tasks, mathematical and real-life problems and investigations occur throughout	Addition and subtraction facts – 14 to 20 Whole numbers to 100 Place value to 99 using structured material Addition and subtraction of two-digit numbers (including money) The 50p coin, collections to 99p, the £1 coin Concept of multiplication 2, 3, 4, 5, 10 times tables; Commutative law Concept of division – sharing and grouping Fractions – halves and quarters notation; one half and one quarter of a set Calculator work	Rounding two-digit whole numbers to the nearest ten	Using standard units – length – m, ½m, cm weight – kg, ½kg capacity – litre Concept of one minute Telling the time – minutes past the hour, quarter past and quarter to using analogue and digital displays Simple durations of time

coverage at Level 2

coverage at Level 3

urriculum (England and Wales)

Algebra	Shape and space		Handling data	
	Shape, location and movement	Measures	Collecting, processing, representing, interpreting	Probability
loring number patterns ding missing numbers – - ■ = 10 d and even numbers	Identifying and naming 3D shapes including spheres and pyramids Identifying and naming 2D shapes including pentagons and hexagons Right angles in 2D shapes Turning through right angles		Collecting and processing data – tick sheets and frequency tables Representing data – mapping diagrams, block graphs, Carroll diagrams Interpreting data	Outcomes – impossible, certain, uncertain
ing number patterns for ental calculations ding missing numbers – < ■ = 12 d and even numbers mple function machines olving addition and btraction	Sorting and naming 3D shapes including the triangular prism Faces, edges and corners of 3D shapes One line of symmetry – recognising symmetrical shapes by folding or using a mirror Right angles in 2D shapes Turning through right angles	Finding areas by counting squares	Collecting and processing data – tally sheets and frequency tables Representing data – bar graphs with scaled axes, Carroll diagrams Interpreting data Decision diagrams	Outcomes – likely, very likely, unlikely, very unlikely

Number, Mo

	Problem Solving and Enquiry	Information Handling	Range and Type of Numbers	Money	Add and Subtract	Multiply and Divide	Round Numbers
HEINEMANN MATHEMATICS 2	Problem solving and investigations occur throughout	Collecting and organising data – tally sheets Displaying data – mapping diagrams, bar graphs and Carroll diagrams Interpreting data	Whole numbers to 20 Using a calculator Place value to 20 Whole numbers to 100 Place value to 99 using material Halves and quarters	1p, 2p, 5p, 10p and 20p coins Change from 5p and 10p Collections to 50p	Subtraction facts – 7 to 10 Linking addition and subtraction facts within 10 Addition and subtraction facts – 11 to 13 Calculator work		
HEINEMANN MATHEMATICS 3	Problem solving and investigations occur throughout	Collecting and organising data – tally sheets Displaying data – bar graphs with scaled axes Interpreting data Decision diagrams	Whole numbers to 100 Place value to 99 using structured material Halves and quarters	The 50p coin Collections to 99p Change from 20p and 50p Addition and subtraction within 99p The £1 coin	Addition and subtraction facts –14 to 20 Addition and subtraction of two-digit numbers Calculator work	Concept of multiplication 2, 3, 4, 5, 10 times tables Calculator work Commutative law Concept of division – sharing and grouping	Rounding two-digit whole numbers nearest te

coverage at Level A

coverage at Level B

coverage at Levels C and D

Scotland)

	Measurement						Shape, Position and Movement			
actions rcent- es and tio	Patterns and Sequences	Functions and Equations	Measure and Estimate	Time	Perimeter Formulae Scales		Range of Shapes	Position and Movement	Symmetry	Angle
actions halves and uarters ractical plications)	Simple number sequences to 20 Sequences with shapes Even and odd numbers	Finding missing numbers 5 + ■ = 8	Using non-standard units – length weight area volume	Telling the time – o'clock and half past using analogue and digital displays Days of the week Months of the year			Identifying and naming 3D shapes including spheres and pyramids Identifying and naming 2D shapes including pentagons and hexagons	Position of an object Moving forward and back Turning through a right		Right angles in 2D shapes
actions halves nd uarters otation inding alves and uarters f uantities	Whole number sequences within 100 Sequences with shapes Even and odd numbers	Finding missing numbers 3 × ■ = 12 Simple function machines involving addition and subtraction	Using standard units length –m, ½m, cm weight –kg, ½kg volume – litre Area by counting squares	Concept of one minute Telling the time – minutes past the hour, quarter past and quarter to using analogue and digital displays Simple durations			Identifying and naming the triangular prism Faces, edges and corners of 3D shapes Tiling with shapes	Giving and under-standing instruc-tions for turning through right angles	One line of symmetry – recognising symmetrical shapes by folding or using a mirror	Right angles in 2D shapes

Using the Course

APPROACHES TO LEARNING AND TEACHING

- The teaching model on which the course is based is one where new ideas are introduced through the involvement of the teacher and children in practical activities and discussion. This is usually followed by further practical activities for the children to do by themselves. Written work involving the use of workbooks and textbooks is only attempted after sufficient practical work and discussion have taken place.

- Given this model, the Teacher's Notes is a crucial component of Heinemann Mathematics 3, as it provides suggestions for practical teaching activities and comments on the use of the other materials.

- Teaching by the teacher is essential and cannot be replaced by the use of workbooks, textbooks and resource materials. These materials provide a framework for teaching, a check on what has already been taught, a record of work completed, and new challenges where the children can apply the mathematics they have learned.

- Heinemann Mathematics 3 provides more ideas for pupil activities, workbook and Textbook pages and assessment material than should be attempted by any one child. The teacher should select the most appropriate activities from the materials provided to suit particular groups or individual children.

- Teaching suggestions for each section of mathematics are found in the Teacher's Notes. Some of the activities suggested are structured in as much as they are teacher-directed with follow-up tasks for the children.

  Other tasks are designed to be more child-directed or investigative. These tasks should encourage the children to explore a new mathematical idea using a problem-solving approach. It is likely that children will complete these tasks in different ways and so discussion between teacher and children during and on completion of the task will be required to ensure meaningful learning. The children should also have opportunities to discuss their work amongst themselves.

PLANNING

Starting points

- It is likely that the teacher will identify the mathematical content by referring to national curricular guidelines and the school's programme of study in mathematics. It should be pointed out that the statements of attainment (England and Wales) describe *outcomes* and are not intended to imply that they should be taught in the exact order presented. The Teacher's Notes for Heinemann Mathematics 3 contains references to attainment targets for each section of mathematics. References are also included for associated workbook and Textbook pages.

- Information about the previous experiences of the children can be found by consulting
  - the children's records of achievement
  - the development charts on Pages 8 and 10 which show the work contained in Heinemann Mathematics 2 and 3
  - the record grids on the back cover of each of the workbooks in Heinemann Mathematics 3
  - the Overview at the beginning of each new section of mathematics in the Teacher's Notes

- The introductory pages at the beginning of each section of mathematics in the Teacher's Notes give
  - the aims for the section of work
  - references to the relevant pages in the Teacher's Notes, workbooks and Textbook. They also identify where problem solving, investigations and extension activities can be found.
  - key words and phrases to which the children should be introduced
  - the materials the teacher may wish to collect and have available, including resource cards
  - references to assessment and other material in the Assessment and Resources Pack

- The teacher should read the Teacher's Notes carefully for the chosen section of mathematics and select the activities which are most appropriate for the children's needs. These activities can be supplemented or replaced, where necessary, by ideas from other sources.

There are a number of activities suggested for introducing and consolidating each mathematical idea. It is unlikely that the children will need to experience all of these.

Routes through the material

Heinemann Mathematics 3 has been designed to be used in a flexible manner. There are many routes through the material. The important principle is to use the sections on number in Workbooks 1 and 2 in the order given and to 'slot in' sections from the Measure, Shape and Handling data Workbook, thus providing a balanced programme of study to suit the needs of the children. The sections from the Measure, Shape and Handling data Workbook need not be tackled in the order given nor indeed should all the work of a particular section, for example, Time, be tackled at any one time.

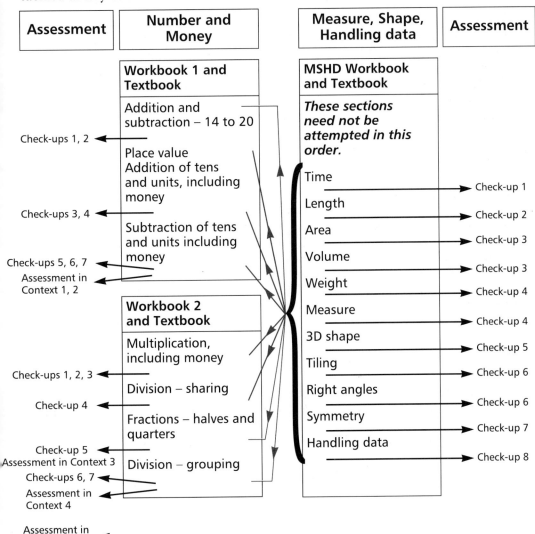

Differentiation

■ There will be times when the teacher will wish to work with the whole class or with individual children. For most activities, however, working with groups of children will be appropriate to allow the teacher to teach and to differentiate work. The teaching suggestions in the Teacher's Notes contain activities for group teaching which might be adapted for use with the whole class or individuals.

■ The following features of Heinemann Mathematics 3 can help the teacher to plan differentiated programmes:
   - suggestions in the Teacher's Notes for practical activities, additional activities and oral work
   - extension activities in both the workbooks and Textbook
   - 'Other activity' pages in the Textbook
   - additional problem solving activities and resource cards in the Assessment and Resources Pack.

■ The teacher should omit pages of the workbooks and Textbook which are not appropriate for particular children. While the extension activities are likely to be used by the more able children, the problem solving and investigation activities are intended to be used by most of the children.

■ The children's progress through the materials is determined by their understanding of the mathematical ideas and should not be planned on the basis of 'a page a day'. Children should have suitable experience of practical activities such as those suggested in the sections on introductory activities in the Teacher's Notes, before attempting to complete workbook or Textbook pages.

Contexts

■ An important consideration in planning is the use of contexts to make the mathematics more meaningful and motivating for the children. Heinemann Mathematics 3 contains a range of contexts through which sections of mathematics are introduced and developed. Suggestions for introducing and developing these contexts are given in the Teacher's Notes. Many of these could be developed across other areas of the curriculum. Some of these extended contexts are listed below:

Workbook 1	Addition and subtraction 14 to 20	Mystery Tour
	Place value, addition and subtraction of tens and units	Adventure World
Workbook 2	Concept of multiplication 2, 3, 4, 5, 10 times tables	School
	Division and fractions	Holiday

■ Some contexts are short scenarios which cover one or two pages of a workbook or the Textbook, for example,

Measure, Shape and Handling data Workbook	Weight	Fruit and vegetable shop

■ Many of the activities in the Teacher's Notes are also contextualised and also involve the use of materials.

ORGANISING AND IMPLEMENTING

Organising the materials

■ At the beginning of each section of work in the Teacher's Notes, the materials required for the workbook, Textbook and introductory activities relating to that section are listed under the heading 'Resources'. Materials from this list, for a particular page or group of pages, should be easily accessible to the children.

■ Teachers should take particular note of the calculator and structured materials symbols which appear on certain pages. These indicate that these items are necessary for particular questions.

■ Exercise books should be available to the children for the work of the Textbook pages and for the questions in the workbooks which have the exercise book symbol.

■ Particular resource cards from the Assessment and Resources Pack should be prepared in advance. These cards can be used to help with a particular aspect of teaching or to provide supplementary activities for individuals or small groups. The notes with these cards describe how they relate to the workbooks or Textbook and how they should be used.

USING THE MATERIALS

■ Introductory teaching, including related practical work, should be carried out before asking the children to attempt the workbook or Textbook pages. The teaching suggestions in the Teacher's Notes have, for the most part, been designed for group teaching and should be adapted to whole class teaching where this is thought to be more appropriate for a particular activity. Practical activities, suggested in the Teacher's Notes, for the children to attempt by themselves, individually or in small groups, should also precede written work.

■ Having undertaken appropriate practical activities it is important for the teacher to 'talk over' workbook and Textbook pages with the children so that they know
  – what they have to do
  – where to find any materials they may need
  – the meaning of any symbols (e.g. calculator) on the page
  – whether they need an exercise book
  – how to record their work
  – which questions they should omit, if any.

Extension activities in the workbooks and Textbook are usually for more able children and can safely be omitted by other pupils.

■ Problem solving and investigative questions on the workbook and Textbook pages are intended for most pupils. Such work can be tackled in small groups where the children discuss ways of *starting* the problem. The teacher can then ask them to explain the strategies they intend to use. When the children are *doing* the problem, the teacher's role is to observe their progress and offer help if asked for or if the group is obviously in difficulties and cannot progress. Such help should be limited so that the children are still left to do their own 'mathematical thinking'. *Reporting* of what the children did and what they found out can often be done orally to other groups or to the whole class.

The Problem Solving Activities booklet in the Assessment and Resources Pack provides 'stand alone' problems for use with individuals or small groups. These problems can be attempted at any time as long as the children understand the mathematics involved. They are concerned with developing simple strategies and mathematical thinking skills.

- 'Other activity' pages (see Page 2) can be used in different ways. For example, a particular page may be attempted by a whole group or alternatively as an additional activity for an individual.

ASSESSING AND RECORDING

Day-to-day assessment

- Much of the assessment of children's learning in the primary classroom is continuous. Many of the everyday tasks that the children are involved in, such as practical tasks, workbook and textbook tasks, and so on, provide evidence which the teacher may use to help establish the level at which a particular child is working. This evidence may be gathered over a period by talking with the children, observing them working and noting how successfully they are able to record their responses. The evidence can be used to identify particular strengths and weaknesses so that future teaching can be made more effective.

Check-ups

- On some occasions the teacher may wish to set a more specific task to check on the child's understanding of a particular piece of mathematics. The check-ups in the Assessment and Resources Pack can be used to do this, usually after each unit of work outlined below has been completed.

- The mathematical topics covered by the check-ups are as follows:

Workbook 1 Number	Workbook 2 Number	MSHD Workbook
1 +, – facts for 14, 15	1 Concept of multiplication 2, 3 times tables	1 Time
2 + and –, 16 to 20	2 4, 5, 10 times tables	2 Length, m and cm
3 Place value, Addition of TU	3 £1 coin and 2, 3, 4, 5 and 10 times tables	3 Area and Volume
4 Adding 3 numbers Money to 99p	4 Division – sharing	4 Weight and Choosing units
5 Subtraction from TU	5 Halves and quarters	5 3D shape – faces, edges, corners
6 Money – change from 20p 50p, +, – to 99p	6 Division – grouping	6 Tiling, right angles, turning
7 + and, –, tens and units	7 ×, ÷, halves and quarters	7 Symmetry
		8 Handling data

- Some of the check-ups involve practical work. Each check-up is referenced to attainment targets and usually covers one or two statements of attainment. The evidence gathered from the check-ups, combined with information from other sources including the teacher's daily observations, can help to identify weaknesses and assist in planning future work.

- A class record guide is include with the notes for the check-ups in the Assessment and Resources Pack.

Assessment in Context

- The notes for teachers in the Assessment in Context booklet indicate mathematical content and attainment targets, give advice about how and when the contexts might be used, and also provide answers.

- Each of the five contexts covers several mathematical topics and a range of attainment targets. Grids which reference individual questions to targets and levels are provided.

- The contexts are intended to help teachers to check on the children's progress and on their ability to apply the mathematics they have met while using the workbooks and Textbook of Heinemann Mathematics 3. Some of the questions involve the children in using problem solving skills.

Problem Solving Activities

- The activities from the booklet in the Assessment and Resources Pack can be used to assess the children's problem solving skills with particular reference to National Curriculum Attainment Target 1 (England and Wales) and the Problem Solving and Enquiry Outcome in Mathematics 5–14 (Scotland).

Record Keeping

- The back cover of each workbook contains a record keeping grid which shows each workbook and Textbook page associated with a mathematical topic. 'Other activity' pages, Check-ups and Assessment in Context are also shown. These grids could be used to show when work has been completed or in a more qualitative way, to show how well a child had performed, for example, by using a number or letter grade.

- The Resource Cards also contain simple checklists for the attainment targets at Levels 2/3 for England and Wales, and for Level B in Scotland. Space is provided to note work which has been attempted or the quality of the performance of individuals or groups.

- The Check-ups and the Assessment in Context contain their own charts and record grids.

Workbook 1: Record of Work   HEINEMANN MATHEMATICS 3

Name _____   Class _____

Addition and subtraction to 20	W1 W2
Addition and subtraction facts for 14 and 15	W3 W4 W5 W6 W7 W8 W9 W10 Check-up 1
Addition and subtraction facts for 16, 17 and 18	W11 W12 W13 W14 W15 W16
Addition and subtraction facts to 20	W17 W18 T1 T2 Check-up 2
Handling data	T3
Other activities	T4 T5
Tens and units: place value, rounding	W19 W20
Addition of tens and units	W21 W22 W23 W24 Check-up 3 W25 W26 T6 T7 T8
Money: the 50p coin, collections to 99p	W27 W28 W29 W30 Check-up 4
Subtraction of tens and units	W31 W32 W33 W34 T9 T10 T11 T12 Check-up 5
Money: change, addition and subtraction to 99p	W35 W36 W37 W38 Check-up 6
Addition and subtraction within 99	T13 T14 Check-up 7
Other activities	T15 T16

▢ indicates that the page, or part of the page, contains problem solving work.

Assessment Context 1   The Bus Journey   ▢
Assessment Context 2   ▢

This workbook is divided into three mathematical sections. Details of the content, resources and language for each section are given at the start of the notes for that section. Each section has its own separate Overview. The three sections are:

	Teacher's Notes
Addition and subtraction facts for 14 to 20	pages 22–41
Addition of tens and units	pages 44–61
Subtraction of tens and units	pages 62–79

The mathematics in the workbook is set within two contexts:

- *Mystery Tour* where a group of children go by bus to different places and events. This is the first part of the workbook and involves mainly addition and subtraction facts for 14 to 20.

- *Adventure World* where the children are involved in different activities in a leisure and recreation park. This is presented in the second part of the workbook and deals with addition and subtraction of tens and units.

Workbook 1

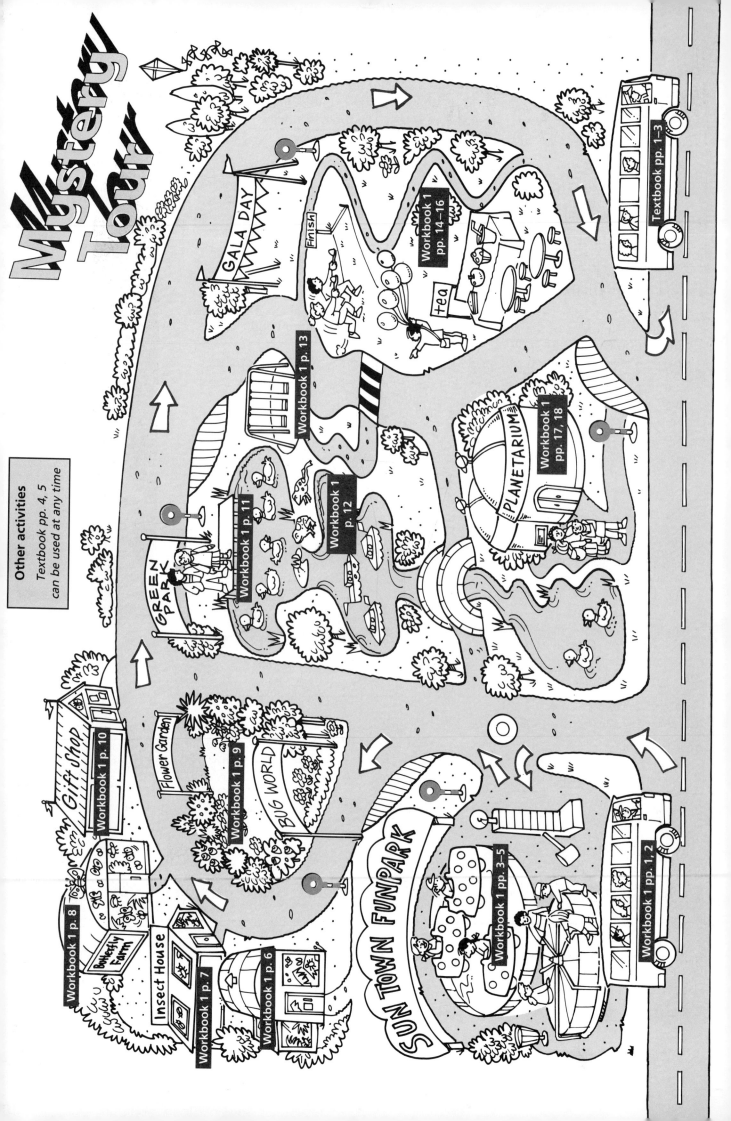

Mystery Tour

Other activities
Textbook pp. 4, 5 can be used at any time

Textbook pp. 1–3

GALA DAY

Finish

Workbook 1 pp. 14–16

tea

Workbook 1 p. 13

PLANETARIUM

Workbook 1 pp. 17, 18

GREEN PARK

Workbook 1 p. 11

Workbook 1 p. 12

Gift Shop

Flower Garden

Workbook 1 p. 10

Workbook 1 p. 9

BUG WORLD

Butterfly Farm

Insect House

Workbook 1 p. 8

Workbook 1 p. 7

Workbook 1 p. 6

SUN TOWN FUNPARK

Workbook 1 pp. 3–5

Workbook 1 pp. 1, 2

Mystery Tour

Setting the scene

The work on Pages 1–18 of Workbook 1 and on associated Textbook pages is set in the context of a 'Mystery Tour' where a group of children travel by bus to a variety of destinations and events:

- Sun Town Funpark
- Bug World
- Green Park
- Gala Day
- Planetarium

These are shown on the map on Page 20 opposite, together with references to the appropriate workbook and Textbook pages.

Introducing the context

Before any mathematics is introduced the scene should be set so that the children have some understanding of the idea of travelling by bus to a number of 'surprise' destinations.

- One way might be to use a poster advertising a mystery tour.

You could ask questions such as

> 'What is a mystery tour?'
> 'Who has been on a mystery tour?'
> 'Where might you go?'
> 'What might you see?'
> 'On what day is the mystery tour?'
> 'At what time does the bus leave?'

Join our Mystery Tour on Wednesday.

The bus will leave at half past 10.

- Preparations for the journey could be discussed. For example,

> 'What clothes would you wear?'
> 'What sort of food would you take? A picnic?' and so on.

- A large picture of the bus with paintings of children at the windows could be created by using the children's paintings of themselves. This bus, or one produced by the teacher, could then be used in conjunction with a large frieze.

As each place is visited, the bus could be moved on and the place name introduced. The children could add drawings to show what happened at each place. The mathematics arising could also be highlighted. The map on Page 20 could be used as the basis for a large chart made up using children's drawings.

Ma 1/2bc
Ma 1/3abd
Ma 2/2ab
Ma 2/3a
Ma 3/2ab
Ma 3/3b
Ma 5/2a
RTN/A1
M/A1
AS/A1, B1
PS/B1
FE/B1, C1
C/B2
D/B2
I/A1, B1
PSE

Addition and subtraction to 20

Overview

This section

- revises addition and subtraction to 20 using materials
- systematically introduces and consolidates addition and subtraction facts for 14, 15, 16, 17, 18, 19 and 20
- includes money and calculator work.

	Teacher's Notes	Workbook 1	Textbook
Addition and subtraction to 20 using materials			
Introductory activities	24	1, 2	
Addition and subtraction facts for 14			
Introductory activities	26	3–5	
Consolidation	28		
Addition and subtraction facts for 15			
Introductory activities	30	6–8	
Consolidation	31		
Calculator work	32	9–10	
Addition and subtraction facts for 16			
Introductory activities	33	11–13	
Consolidation	35		
Addition and subtraction facts for 17 and 18			
Introductory activities	36	14–16	
Addition and subtraction facts for 19 and 20			
Introductory activities	37	17	
Addition and subtraction facts to 20			
Consolidation	38	18	1, 2
Handling data			3
Other activities			4, 5
Extension			1, 2, 5
Investigation		3, 6, 11	
Problem solving		4, 9, 10, 12, 15, 16	2, 5

Key words and phrases

complete	even	code
copy and complete	difference between	machine

Resources

Useful materials

- small objects for counting such as beads, counters, bricks, buttons
- interlocking cubes
- 1p, 5p, 10p coins
- coloured pencils
- calculators
- squared paper
- other materials suggested within the introductory activities
- flashcards of key words and phrases

Assessment and Resources Pack

Assessment

Check-ups

Check-up 1
Workbook 1 Pages 1–10
(+ and – facts for 14, 15)

Check-up 2
Workbook 1 Pages 11–18
(+ and – facts for 16 to 20)

Resources

Problem Solving Activities

1 Train tracks (Number patterns)
2 Lighting up (Calculator digits)
3 Rows and columns (Addition of 3 numbers, totals <10)

Resource Cards

Resource Cards 1 to 3 (Day out) involve addition facts 14 to 20.

Resource Cards 4 to 7 (Bus trip) involve subtraction facts 14 to 20.

Teaching notes

ADDITION AND SUBTRACTION TO 20 USING MATERIALS
Introductory activities

Ma 2/3a 2/2b
RTN/A1 AS/B1

Practical activities in adding and subtracting within 20 were introduced in Heinemann Mathematics 2, Workbook 4. These were followed by the detailed study of addition and subtraction facts for 11, 12 and 13. Suggestions for further practical adding and subtracting activities within 20 are given now, before detailed studies of number facts for 14 to 20 are considered.

The following activities are all related to buses and should involve you and a group of children in practical work and discussion. A selection could be made from these suggestions.

1 Bus passengers
Cubes could be used to represent passengers on a large cardboard bus.

■ 'There are 8 passengers on the bus. 11 more get on. How many are there altogether?'

The answer is found by counting on in ones. The teacher or child writes 8 + 11 = 19.

Repeat for other numbers.

■ 'There are 17 people on the bus. 9 get off. How many are left?'

The answer is found by removing 9 cubes from 17 cubes. The teacher or child writes 17 − 9 = 8.

Repeat for other numbers.

2 Loading and unloading the boot
An open cardboard box could be used for the boot, and two colours of cubes or counters to represent two different colours of cases.

■ To load the boot, the children could pick a card showing an addition, for example, 9+8

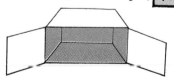

'Put 9 brown cases and 8 blue cases in the boot. How many cases are there altogether?'

Write 9 + 8 = 17

■ To unload the boot, the children could pick a card showing a subtraction, for example, $\boxed{17-5}$

'Put 17 cases in the boot. Take out 5. How many are left?'

Write 17 − 5 = 12

3 The bus carpet

A large number strip made from wallpaper could be placed on the floor. The children move up and down the bus.

'Stand on 5. Move up 9.'

Write 5 + 9 = 14

'Stand on 16. Move down 7.'

Write 16 − 7 = 9

The children could take turns, giving instructions and writing down the appropriate number story.

4 Seat numbers

A supply of tickets is needed for this activity. Each ticket gives a different answer to represent a seat number, for example,

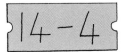 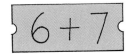 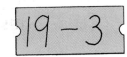 and so on.

Each child chooses a ticket, finds the answer and states or writes what seat number this represents.

20
19
18
17
16
15
14
13
12
11
10
9
8
7
6
5
4
3
2
1

Workbook 1

Ma 2/3a
AS/B1 RTN/B1

Workbook 1 Pages 1 and 2   *Addition and subtraction to 20*

The children are expected to find the answers by placing counting materials on each page. On Page 1 Question 3, the back seat of the bus contains 5 children, all of whom have the same ticket number, 13. Some of these children's names appear in scenarios on subsequent pages.

ADDITION AND SUBTRACTION FACTS FOR 14 TO 20

This section examines the addition and subtraction facts for each of the numbers 14 to 20 in turn. Emphasis is given to certain related addition and subtraction facts as these will have to be memorised. For example,

$$9 + 5 = 14 \qquad 14 - 5 = 9$$
$$5 + 9 = 14 \qquad 14 - 9 = 5$$

Examples such as $13 + 6 = 19$ and $18 - 5 = 13$, which need not be memorised, are considered later in Workbook 1 (Pages 21 and 31) in the sections on addition and subtraction of tens and units.

It is important that practical work and discussion between you and the children and among the children themselves take place before they start written work. Practical activities are suggested for each of the number stories from 14 to 20. While these activities are described for a specific number, they can be adapted and used for the other numbers.

To help memorise these facts, oral work, games and activities should play an important part in the children's learning experience. Suggestions about these are given within these notes.

ADDITION AND SUBTRACTION FACTS FOR 14
Introductory activities

Ma 2/3a 2/2b
AS/B1 RTN/A1

Sun Town Funpark

This is the first stop on the Mystery Tour. Discuss what happens at a funpark and list the activities which the children particularly like. Drawings and pictures could be added to the ongoing frieze or chart. The children could count the number of letters in 'Sun Town Funpark' and be told that at this funpark many of the activities involve the number 14.

The following activities involve practical work and discussion for you and the children. A selection could be made from these.

1 Dodgems *(addition facts)*

The vertical layout is suggested here to mirror Workbook 1, Page 3. This layout was introduced in Heinemann Mathematics 2.

Use 14 cars or cubes and a drawing of a dodgem area.

'Put some cars above and below the line as shown.'

Write
$$\begin{array}{r} 6 \\ + 8 \\ \hline 14 \end{array}$$

Find other facts, in particular,

$$\begin{array}{r} 10 \\ + 4 \\ \hline \end{array} \qquad \begin{array}{r} 9 \\ + 5 \\ \hline \end{array} \qquad \begin{array}{r} 8 \\ + 6 \\ \hline \end{array} \qquad \begin{array}{r} 7 \\ + 7 \\ \hline \end{array} \qquad \begin{array}{r} 6 \\ + 8 \\ \hline \end{array} \qquad \begin{array}{r} 5 \\ + 9 \\ \hline \end{array} \qquad \begin{array}{r} 4 \\ + 10 \\ \hline \end{array}$$

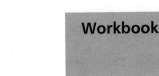

2 Coconuts *(subtraction facts)*

Put 14 coconuts (paper cups) in a line.

'Knock down 4. How many are left?'

The answer is found by counting the paper cups.
A child could record the story on a score card.

3 Ghost Train *(subtraction facts)*

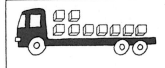 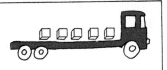

'The Ghost Train has 14 carriages. 4 carriages are hidden in the tunnel.' (Cover with a strip of card.)

'How many carriages are not in the tunnel?'

Write 14 − 4 = 10

Repeat for other numbers and write
14 − 5 = 9
14 − 6 = 8
14 − 7 = 7
14 − 8 = 6
14 − 9 = 5
14 − 10 = 4

4 Loading the dodgems on to lorries *(related facts)*

Provide a chart with cut-outs of a blue and a red lorry. Use 14 cars or cubes. Put some on each lorry, for example, 9 and 5.

Write 9 + 5 = 14
5 + 9 = 14

'If the blue lorry moves off, how many cars are left?'

Write 14 − 9 = 5

'If the red lorry moves off, how many cars are left?'

Write 14 − 5 = 9

Repeat for other related facts.

5 Individual activities *(related facts)*

■ Use 14 cubes or counters, partition the set and write stories, for example,

10 + 4 = 14   14 − 4 = 10
4 + 10 = 14   14 − 10 = 4

■ Put 14 beads on a string and divide them into two sets.

Write 9 + 5 = 14
5 + 9 = 14
14 − 5 = 9
14 − 9 = 5

The related subtraction facts can be found by covering the 5 beads and then the 9 beads.

■ Use 14 pegs of two colours and a pegboard.

Write   7 + 7 = 14
           14 − 7 = 7

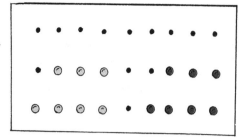

Ma 2/3a 3/2b 1/2c 1/3a
AS/B1 RTN/A1 FE/B1 PSE

Investigation

Problem solving

Workbook 1 Pages 3 to 5   *Addition and subtraction facts for 14*

On Page 3, make sure the children realise there are 14 lights on the car. In Question 4, explain the use of the exercise book symbol. This is the first time the children have met this.

The idea of 3 + □ = 5 or '3 and what is 5' was introduced in Heinemann Mathematics 2.

On Page 4, Question 1, examples of type 8 + □ = 14 are answered from a diagram. Some children may need help in using the diagram. In Question 2, the children may find it helpful to score off each fish as it is taken from the tank. In Question 3, the children should be encouraged to find as many solutions as they can.

On Page 5, some of the children introduced on Pages 1 and 2 are shown buying tickets for certain activities. In Question 2, the name of the place visited and the cost should be entered on each ticket. For example,

Bikes 4p

ADDITION AND SUBTRACTION FACTS FOR 14
Consolidation

Ma 2/3a 2/2b 3/2ab
AS/B1 RTN/A1 FE/B1

1   Oral work

Regular oral work is important in helping children to memorise and recall addition and subtraction facts. A variety of language should be used. For example,

'What is 9 add 5?

What is 14 take away 7? 14 subtract 8?

Find the difference between 14 and 5.

Give me two numbers which add to 14; another two.

9 and what make 14?

What number is 5 more than 9? 6 less than 14?

A toffee apple cost 8p and a stick of rock 6p. How much is that altogether?

I had 14p. I bought a toffee apple costing 8p. How much had I left?

A pencil cost 14p and a rubber 9p. What is the difference in price?'

The children could also be asked to make up their own problems for a given fact such as 10+ 4 or 14 − 6.

2 Find the dodgems

A chart could be prepared with dodgem flag poles numbered from 4 to 10,

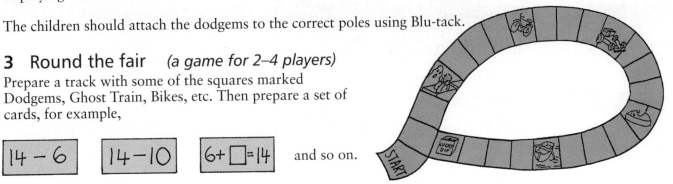

together with a set of dodgems
displaying subtractions:

The children should attach the dodgems to the correct poles using Blu-tack.

3 Round the fair   *(a game for 2–4 players)*

Prepare a track with some of the squares marked
Dodgems, Ghost Train, Bikes, etc. Then prepare a set of
cards, for example,

     and so on.

In turn each player takes a card and moves forward the number of squares given by
the answer, which can be checked using a calculator. If the answer is wrong, the
player does not move. If the counter lands on a square like Ghost Train the player
gets a free ride and collects a counter. The winner could be the player who has
collected most free rides after a given time or the first player to collect four (or any
other number of) free rides.

4 Clown's hat

Draw a picture of a clown's hat, as shown, with '14'
on the brim and spaces for 2 number cards to be
positioned above. Prepare number cards, 4 to 10.

One child puts a card in the bottom part of the hat.
The other child has to pick a card for the top part of
the hat so that the total is 14. The total of the two
cards can be checked on a calculator.

5 Playing cards

Select a suit and use cards 4 to 10.

One child picks a card and the other has to pick another card so that the total is 14,
for example,

Totals can be checked on a calculator.

7 Story card

This card could be put on display.

It summarises the addition facts for 14.

$\underset{\bullet}{7}$ indicates that 7 + 7 = 14.

The card could also be used for subtraction facts. For example, for 14 − 5, following the loop from 5 gives the answer, 9.

ADDITION AND SUBTRACTION FACTS FOR 15
Introductory activities

Ma 2/2b 2/3a 3/2b 1/2c
AS/B1 RTN/A1 FE/B1

Bug World

This is the second stop on the Mystery Tour, where various insects are seen. During their stay, the children visit the gift shop to buy souvenir badges. The scene could be set by asking who has been to an insect farm and what they saw. Drawings and pictures, including the children's own designs for badges, could be added to the ongoing frieze or chart and the bus moved to this new location.

Most of the activities involve the number 15. Perhaps the children could invent a name for this location, using 15 letters, for example, 'Bengie's Bug World'.

Some introductory practical activities for teacher and children working together are given below. An appropriate selection could be made from these.

1 Bugs on leaves   (addition facts)

Two large green leaves, one above the other, could be drawn on a piece of paper and 15 counters used to represent bugs. Place the bugs on the leaves and write stories such as

$$\begin{array}{c}10\\+5\\\hline 15\end{array} \qquad \begin{array}{c}9\\+6\\\hline 15\end{array} \qquad \begin{array}{c}8\\+7\\\hline 15\end{array} \qquad \begin{array}{c}7\\+8\\\hline 15\end{array} \qquad \begin{array}{c}6\\+9\\\hline 15\end{array} \qquad \begin{array}{c}5\\+10\\\hline 15\end{array}$$

The vertical layout is suggested here to mirror that used in Workbook 1, Page 6.

2 Bugs in a box   (subtraction facts)

Put 15 bugs (counters) in a shallow box.

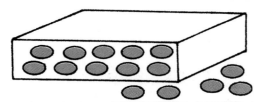

'5 escape. How many are left?'

Write   15 − 5 = 10

'6 escape. How many are left?'

Write   15 − 6 = 9

and so on.

3 Nature trail   (complementary addition)

A large number strip to 15 could be prepared.

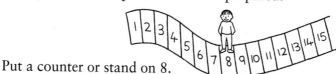

Put a counter or stand on 8.

30

'How many more steps to reach 15?'

Write $8 + \square = 15$

$8 + \boxed{7} = 15$

Repeat for other starting points from 5 to 10.

4 Ladybirds   *(related facts)*

A large cardboard ladybird could be drawn and 15 counters used to represent spots.
Put spots on either side of the dividing line.

Write $7 + 8 = 15$
$8 + 7 = 15$

By covering up or removing spots, the related
subtraction facts can be found.

Write $15 - 8 = 7$
$15 - 7 = 8$

5 Individual activities   *(related facts)*

The individual activities outlined for the story of 14 (see Page 26) can be adapted
for the story of 15.

Interlocking cubes

   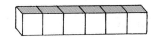

Write $9 + 6 = 15$
$6 + 9 = 15$

Take away 6 cubes. 9 are left.

Write $15 - 6 = 9$

Take away 9 cubes. 6 are left.

Write $15 - 9 = 6$

| Ma 2/2b 2/3a 3/2a |
| AS/B1 RTN/A1 PS/B1 |

Investigation

Workbook 1 Pages 6 to 8   *Addition and subtraction facts for 15*

On Page 6, Question 2, the children are expected to find other number stories
by distributing the 15 counters between the two webs at the top of the page. In
Question 3, the children should write answers in the white rectangle.

On Page 7, Question 4 refers to even numbers. These were introduced in
Heinemann Mathematics 2 as the series of numbers 2, 4, 6, 8, etc. The children
may need to be reminded about this.

On Page 8, the children should be encouraged to find answers without using
material.

ADDITION AND SUBTRACTION FACTS FOR 15
Consolidation

1 Oral work

For the story of 15 work similar to that indicated for the story of 14 should be
carried out (see Page 28).

| Ma 2/2b 2/3a 1/2b |
| AS/B1 RTN/A1 FE/B1 |

Other suggestions are

■ using flashcards, for example,

■ using a story card to elicit related facts. For example,

$$5 + 10 = 15$$
$$10 + 5 = 15$$
$$15 - 10 = 5$$
$$15 - 5 = 10 \quad \text{and so on.}$$

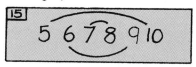

2 Nature trail

You will need:

– a track similar to that outlined on Page 29, with some squares marked Butterflies, Ants, Moths, Wasps, etc.

– a set of cards of type   and so on.

The game is played as before, but this time the players collect counters which represent insects.

3 Worm cards

You will need:

– a set of worm cards in two different colours (e.g. yellow and blue) as shown below.

Yellow

Blue

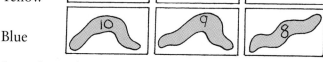

Spread out the cards, face down. A child picks up a yellow one and a blue one. If a matching pair is obtained, then the child keeps both cards. If not, the cards are replaced, face down. The winner is the child with most pairs.

4 Worms in apples

Prepare a set of apple cards 5 to 10 and a set of worm cards, 5 to 10.

A child picks a worm card, for example, 5. To eat the apple, the worm has to be attached to the apple card, in this case 10, so that the total of the two numbers is 15.

ADDITION AND SUBTRACTION TO 15
Calculator work: Introductory activities

Ma 2/2b 2/3a 1/2b
AS/B1

The calculator was introduced in Heinemann Mathematics 2 for a variety of activities involving addition and subtraction. It would be worthwhile checking that the children remember how to key in numbers, how to use the ⊞ ⊟ and ⊟ keys, and how to clear the display.

Question 1, Workbook 1, Page 9 deals with an aspect of addition and subtraction which was first introduced in the Calculator Workcards of Heinemann Mathematics 2. Some children may not be familiar with these cards and so some preliminary teaching could be done as follows:

1 Adding on

'Enter 5 in your calculator. You have to make 5 become 8.
Is 8 larger or smaller than 5? (*Larger*)
Will you add or subtract? (*Add*)
What will you add ? (*3*)'

Press $\boxed{+}$ $\boxed{3}$ $\boxed{=}$ to give 8.

Repeat for other numbers.

2 Subtracting

'Enter 9 in your calculator. You have to make 9 become 7.
Is 7 larger or smaller than 9? (*Smaller*)
Will you add or subtract? (*Subtract*)
What will you subtract?(*2*)'

Press $\boxed{-}$ $\boxed{2}$ $\boxed{=}$ to give 7.

Repeat for other numbers.

Note: You may wish to introduce the language 'plus' for the $\boxed{+}$ key and 'minus' for the $\boxed{-}$ key at this point.

Workbook 1 Pages 9 and 10   *Addition and subtraction to 15: Calculator work and money*

Ma 2/2b 2/3a 1/3a 3/2b 5/2a
AS/B1 I/A1 FE/B1

Some preliminary work as outline above should be carried out before the children try Page 9, Question 1. Make sure the children realise they have to go from flower to flower. For example,

'Go from 9 to 15. Enter 9 in the calculator. Will you add or subtract? What will you add? Try it' and so on.

Question 2 involves finding the answers to subtractions and interpreting the graph to find what flower is represented by each of these answers. Interpreting such a graph was introduced in Heinemann Mathematics 2.

Page 10 contains addition and subtraction of money to 15p. In Question 1, the children have each bought two badges which they are wearing. There are several answers to the first part of Question 3. For example two ants (12p) or a wasp and a ladybird (13p) as well as pairs that cost exactly 14p. The children should be asked to explain their answer to the second part of Question 3.

Problem solving

Problem solving

ADDITION AND SUBTRACTION FACTS FOR 16
Introductory activities

Green Park

Ma 2/3a
AS/B1 RTN/A1

The next stop on the Mystery Tour is Green Park which has different areas such as a pond and a playpark. It would be useful to have a large drawing of a pond in a park which could be used as indicated later.

Various practical activities are suggested below and a selection could be made from these.

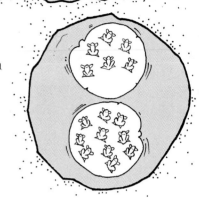

1 Frogs (addition facts)

Place two large lily pads on the pond. Use 16 counters, cubes or cut-out frogs. Arrange the 16 frogs on the lily pads as shown.

Write   7 + 9 = 16

Repeat for other arrangements of 16 frogs.

Vary the position of the lily pads so that the children could also use the vertical setting.

Write
$$
\begin{array}{r}
6 \\
+\,10 \\
\hline
16
\end{array}
$$

2 Frogs (subtraction facts)

Put the 16 frogs on the bank of the pond.

   '9 jump into the pond. How many are left?'

Write   16 − 9 = 7   or
$$
\begin{array}{r}
16 \\
-\ 9 \\
\hline
7
\end{array}
$$

Repeat for other numbers of frogs jumping into the pond.

3 Frogs (related facts)

Place one lily pad on the pond. Put 7 frogs on the lily pad and 9 in the water.

Write the stories   7 + 9 = 16
                     9 + 7 = 16
                    16 − 7 = 9
                    16 − 9 = 7

Repeat for other arrangements of 16 frogs.

4 Model boats (related facts)

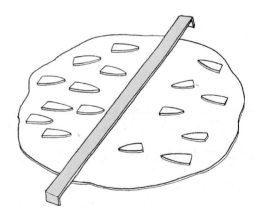

Use cubes, counters or cut-out pictures of boats. Make a bridge over the pond. Arrange the 16 boats on either side of the bridge as shown.

Write the stories   9 + 7 = 16
                     7 + 9 = 16
                    16 − 7 = 9
                    16 − 9 = 7

Repeat for other arrangements of 16 boats.

5 Boat race (related facts)

Make a starting line for a boat race. Use a string and 16 beads, 6 red and 10 yellow.

Write   6 + 10 = 16
        10 + 6 = 16

The related subtraction facts can be found by removing one colour of bead from the string or separating the two colours.

Write 16 − 6 = 10
       16 − 10 = 6

Repeat for 9 red beads and 7 yellow beads, and so on.

6 Boat race *(addition facts)*

Make a badge for the winner of a boat race. Use two colours and squared paper with 16 squares as shown below.

 or

The children should colour squares to show a number fact for 16.

For example, these badges each show 9 + 7 = 16.

Other badges could show 8 + 8 = 16 and 10 + 6 = 16.

Workbook Pages 11 to 13   *Addition and subtraction facts for 16*

Ma 2/2b 2/3a 3/2b
AS/B1 RTN/A1 FE/B1 PSE

On Page 11, Question 2, the children may well write answers such as

     11
    + 5   and this of course, should be accepted.
     ___
     16

The particular facts which have to be memorised are practised on Page 12, Questions 1 and 2.

On Page 11, Question 4, the children are asked to find three numbers which add to 16.

Investigation

On Page 12, Question 4, the children are expected to key in, for example, ⑨ ⊞ and then try a number for ☐. If necessary, they then try again, and adjust the ☐ number accordingly to make 16.

Problem solving

ADDITION AND SUBTRACTION FACTS TO 16
Consolidation

1 Kite-flying exhibition *(addition facts)*

Ma 2/2b 2/3a 1/2b
AS/B1 RTN/A1 FE/B1

The children could make a set of kites. Put the number 14, 15 or 16 on each.

Ask the children to find a number fact related to the number on the kite, record it on a bow and attach it to the string. The kites could be suspended from the ceiling.

2 Oral work

Details given on Pages 28 and 31 could be adapted for the facts to 16, for example,

- using flashcards $\boxed{9+7}$ $\boxed{10+6}$ $\boxed{16-9}$
- using a story card to elicit related facts

ADDITION AND SUBTRACTION FACTS FOR 17 AND 18
Introductory activities

Gala Day

The next stop on the Mystery Tour is a village where a Gala Day is being held. The village is decorated with brightly coloured flags. The bus stops at a park where sports are taking place. At one side of the park there is a tea stall. Some of these features could be illustrated on the frieze or wall chart.

A number of practical activities are suggested below, and a selection could be made from these.

1 Spotty dogs   *(related facts)*

Use two large cut-out dogs with counters for spots. Arrange 17 counters on the two dogs as shown.

Write $7 + 10 = 17$
$10 + 7 = 17$
$17 - 10 = 7$
$17 - 7 = 10$

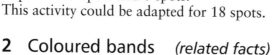

Repeat for 9 spots and 8 spots.
This activity could be adapted for 18 spots.

2 Coloured bands   *(related facts)*

Select 18 children. Give 10 children red bands and 8 children green bands.

Write the stories $10 + 8 = 18$
$8 + 10 = 18$
$18 - 8 = 10$
$18 - 10 = 8$

Repeat this activity with 9 red bands and 9 green bands.

3 Thirsty work   *(addition and subtraction facts)*

Taking part in the races at the Gala Day is thirsty work. A refreshment stall could be set up in the classroom. Different drinks and snacks could have the following prices 7p, 8p, 9p, 9p and 10p. Alternatively, a set of cards with pictures of each item and its price could be used.

- 'What is the cost of and ?
  Write $9p + 8p = 17p$

  'Put out coins to pay for them.' (10p) (5p) (2p)

■ 'You have 18p to spend. Buy  How much have you left?'

Write 18p − 10p = 8p   or

$$\begin{array}{r} 18\text{p} \\ -\ 10\text{p} \\ \hline 8\text{p} \end{array}$$

Workbook 1 Pages 14 to 16   *Addition and subtraction facts for 17 and 18*

On Page 15, Question 2, the children are asked to find 3 tyres which give a total of 17. There are two possible solutions. A calculator could be used to check a solution.

On Page 16, Question 1, the children are expected to find the total cost. They then put out coins for this total before recording in the table.

In Question 3, the children are expected to write a ticket such as | 16−6 | or

| 14−4 | . Some children may, however, write | 5+5 | or | 7+3 | and

this should also be accepted.

ADDITION AND SUBTRACTION FACTS FOR 19 AND 20
Introductory activities

The Planetarium

The final stopping place on this Mystery Tour is the Planetarium. This scenario could be developed by allowing individuals, or small groups of children to imagine what the planets and the creatures and plants on them might look like. These plants and creatures could be used for some of the practical activities.

1   The sky at night   *(related facts)*

A simple background made from black or dark blue paper could be used for this activity. Cut-out stars or planets in two colours are also required.
Put 9 red stars and 10 yellow stars on the paper.

Write   9 + 10 = 19
        10 + 9 = 19
        19 − 10 = 9
        19 − 9 = 10

2   The planet Zol   *(related facts)*

You will need a large cut-out planet and counters or cubes to represent creatures and plants.

   20 creatures – 10 purple, 10 red

   20 plants – 10 green, 10 yellow

- 'Put the 20 creatures on the planet.'

    Write $10 + 10 = 20$
              $20 - 10 = 10$

- 'Put the 20 plants on the planet.'

    Write
$$\begin{array}{r} 10 \\ +\,10 \\ \hline 20 \end{array} \qquad \begin{array}{r} 20 \\ -\,10 \\ \hline 10 \end{array}$$

Ma 2/3a
AS/B1 RTN/A1

Workbook Page 17   *Addition and subtraction facts to 20*

The work on Page 17 reinforces the facts for 19 and 20 and gives general practice in addition and subtraction facts from 14 to 20.

ADDITION AND SUBTRACTION FACTS TO 20
Consolidation

Ma 2/2b 2/3a 3/2b 3/3b 1/3d
AS/B1 RTN/A1 FE/B1,C1

1   Rockets

Draw four separate rockets, each with one of the numbers 17, 18, 19 or 20.

Prepare a set of spacemen, as shown.

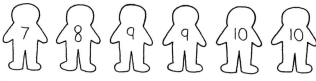

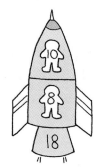

Ask the children to put into the rocket two spacemen whose total is the rocket's number.

The children then write the story, for example $8 + 10 = 18$.

2   Shooting stars

Draw four separate shooting stars, each with one of the numbers 10, 9, 8 or 7.

Prepare a set of subtraction cards as shown.

$17 - 7$	$17 - 8$	$17 - 9$	$17 - 10$	$18 - 8$
$18 - 9$	$18 - 10$	$19 - 9$	$19 - 10$	$20 - 10$

Give the children a shooting star, for example 10. Ask them to place on the star, subtraction cards with an answer of 10.

Repeat for the other stars.

3   Oral activities

Doubles

Most children find doubles easy to remember, for example,

$6 + 6 = 12$, $7 + 7 = 14$, $8 + 8 = 16$, $9 + 9 = 18$, $10 + 10 = 20$.

Using the doubles addition facts

You may wish to investigate 'doubles and one' with children. For example,

'7 and 7 make 14. What will 7 and 8 make?
7 and 7 make 14, so 7 and 8 will be one more, 15.'

4   Function machines

In Heinemann Mathematics 1 and 2 the idea of a 'rule' operating on a number was introduced. This could be expressed in words, for example, 'Add 2', 'Subtract 4' or using symbols, for example, '+ 2' or '– 4'. The results were then expressed as a mapping or arrow diagram. In Workbook 1 this idea is developed to include the notion of a function machine.

Finding the output number

In this activity the children are given an input number and a rule and are asked to find the output number.

The children could work in pairs or as a group. One child could act as a 'number gobbler' with a label round her/his neck showing the planet 'rule', for example 'add 10' and armbands indicating 'IN' and 'OUT'.

Another child in the group could select a number card from 1 to 10 for the 'IN' arm, predict the answer and select the appropriate card from 11 to 20 for the 'OUT' arm of the 'number gobbler'.

This could be recorded as

IN	add 10	OUT
4	⟶	14
1	⟶	11
6	⟶	16

Similar examples could be done for subtraction.

Finding a rule

In this activity the children are given an input number and an output number and asked to find the rule. The children are told the rule is 'add' or 'subtract'.

Given an input number 15 and an output number 8 the children should state the rule 'subtract 7'.

Similar examples could be done for addition.

Making a machine

You might find that an actual model of a machine will motivate the children. The simplest form to make is a decorated box or carton.

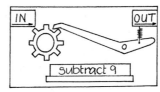

You will need cards for input and output numbers. A child selects an input card, predicts the answer and selects the appropriate output card.

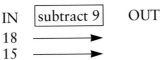

IN	subtract 9	OUT
18	⟶	
15	⟶	

The rule label should be changed and cards used to suit. Later the label can 'fall off' the machine and from the list of input and output numbers, the children have to find the rule.

Workbook 1 Page 18 *Function machines: + and – facts to 20*

Before attempting Page 18, the children should be familiar with how function machines operate.

Textbook Pages 1 and 2 *Using + and – facts to 20*

The Textbook pages continue the Mystery Tour context and reinforce the addition and subtraction facts to 20 using a variety of formats.

Extension

On Page 1, Question 3, the children are asked to write their own number stories to match letters.

For example, R could be $\begin{array}{r} 5 \\ +7 \\ \hline \end{array}$ or $\begin{array}{r} 6 \\ +6 \\ \hline \end{array}$

Problem solving

Extension

On Page 2, Question 4, the children are asked to find a rule for a function machine. This assumes prior teaching and discussion as outlined earlier.

Textbook Page 3 *Handling data*

Page 3 rounds off the Mystery Tour by considering which places the children liked best to visit. Before the children attempt this page, it is important that they have completed the Handling Data Workbook in Heinemann Mathematics 2, or similar work, so that they are familiar with

- interpreting information from a bar graph

- using a Carroll diagram as a means of sorting and displaying information.

Question 5 is a practical activity which could be undertaken by a small group of children. It provides an opportunity for children to apply their knowledge of the handling data process.

Textbook Page 4 *Other activity: addition to 10*

- This activity gives children the opportunity to reinforce addition facts to 10 and could be attempted at any time.

- Ensure that the children are familiar with the format for recording answers i.e. looping the numbers vertically, horizontally but not diagonally.

Questions 1 and 2 consolidate the addition facts of 10 and 9 respectively. After each question it is important to discuss how the children tackled the problem and the strategies used.

Additional activity

Allow the children to create their own number squares to 'make 7' or 'make 8'.

Textbook Page 5 *Other activity: puzzle*

■ This activity gives children the opportunity to use a trial and error strategy for solving problems, and can be attempted at any time.

■ Ensure that the children are familiar with dominoes. Discuss Question 1 with the children to find other ways of making the number rectangle, for example,

Each of the number rectangles in Questions 2(c) and 2(d) has one solution only.

Question 3 should be attempted by only some children.

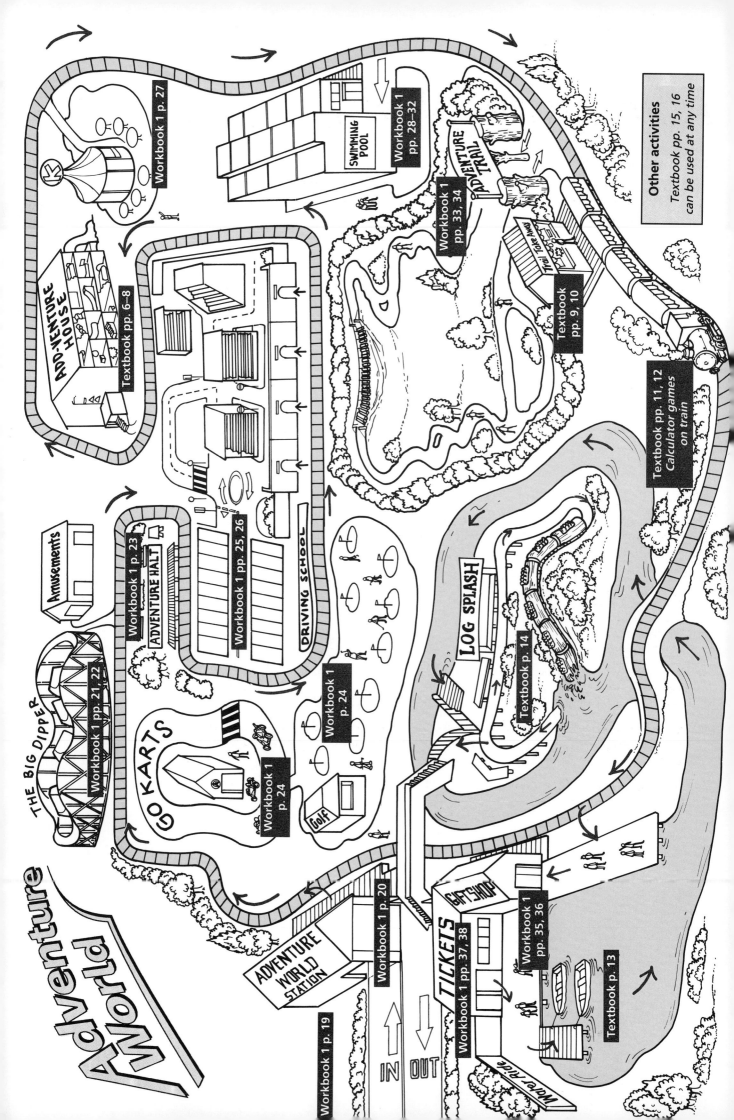

Adventure World

Setting the scene

The work on Pages 20–38 of Workbook 1 and on associated Textbook pages is set in the context of 'Adventure World', where children are involved in the different activities in a leisure and recreation park:

- Big Dipper
- Adventure Halt
- Go-Karts and Golf
- Driving School
- Kiosk
- Swimming Pool
- Adventure Trail
- Gift Shop

These are shown on the map on Page 42 opposite, together with references to the appropriate workbook and Textbook pages.

Introducing the context

Before any mathematics is introduced the scene should be set so that the children have some understanding of the kind of leisure and recreational events on offer in Adventure World.

- You could ask questions such as,

  'What is a leisure or recreation park?'
  'Who has been to a leisure park?'
  'Which one?'
  'What did you do?'

- A drawing or chart showing the various activities could be made and displayed during the work. The children could collect brochures which advertise places similar to Adventure World and these could be displayed and discussed.

- As the work progresses, different aspects of Adventure World would be discussed in more detail so that the children become more familiar with the activities of the park.

- The map on Page 40 could be used as the basis for a large chart made up using children's drawings.

Ma 1/3abd
Ma 2/2ab
Ma 2/3ad
Ma 3/3a
RTN/B1
M/B1
AS/B1,2
RN/B1
PS/B2
PSE

Addition of tens and units

Overview

This section introduces

■ the use of structured material

■ the idea of expressing numbers to the nearest 10

■ adding tens and units

■ the associative law

■ the 50p coin and counting money to 99p.

	Teacher's Notes	Workbook 1	Textbook
Place value to 99			
Revision	46		
Structured material	47	19	
Approximation to the nearest ten	48	20	
Adding units to tens and units			
No carrying	50	21	
With carrying	51	22	
Adding tens and units to tens and units			
No carrying	53	23	
With carrying	54	24	
Adding three single-digit numbers: associative law	55	25	
Addition: problems, language, calculator work	56	26	6–8
Money to 49p	58	27	
The 50p coin and money to 99p	60	28–30	
Money to 99p			
Additional activities	61		
Extension		29	
Problem solving			7, 8

Key words and phrases

tens and units material	column	how much money?
exchange	total	enough money
to the nearest	sum	how much money left?
	plus	

Resources

Useful materials

■ notation cards

■ structured material such as Tillich or Dienes base 10 material

■ dice

■ number line on classroom wall

■ calculators

■ real, plastic or cardboard coins, and purses

■ coin cards

■ other materials suggested within the introductory activities

■ flashcards of key words and phrases

Assessment and Resources Pack

Assessment

Check-ups

Check-up 3
Workbook 1 Pages 19–24
(Place value   Addition of TU)

Check-up 4
Workbook 1 Pages 25–30
(Adding 3 numbers
Money to 99p)

Resources

Problem Solving Activities
4 Car numbers (Numbers to 99)
5 Games (Numbers and prices to 99p)

Resource Cards
Resource Cards 8 and *9* (Which pairs?)
involve adding tens and units.

Teaching notes

PLACE VALUE TO 99
Revision

Ma 2/2a
RTN/B1

A sound knowledge of place value is essential if children are to develop a complete understanding of the techniques of addition and subtraction which follow in this workbook.

Place value to 99 was introduced in Heinemann Mathematics 2 using material such as straws and Unifix cubes. Children should already know that, for example, forty-five = 45 = 4 tens and 5 units and conversely that 4 tens and 5 units = 45.

Some children, however, may benefit by doing some of the following activities.

1 Counting straws

'Count out twenty-five straws. Put them in bundles of ten.'

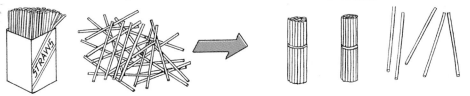

Write   twenty-five = 25 = 2 tens and 5 units

2 Putting beads or marbles into tubs or trays

'Count out thirty-four marbles. Put ten in each tub.'

Write   thirty-four = 34 = 3 tens and 4 units ·

3 Stringing beads

'Count out twenty-six beads. Put ten beads on each string.'

Write   twenty-six = 26 = 2 tens and 6 units

4 Fitting interlocking cubes

'Count out twenty-three cubes. Fit them together in tens.'

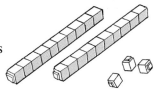

Write   twenty-three = 23 = 2 tens and 3 units

The children are now introduced to structured material such as Tillich or Dienes base 10 material. This material is particularly useful when teaching the techniques of addition and subtraction. Children need time to explore this new material and appreciate that ten units are equivalent to 1 ten.

Ma 2/2a
RTN/B1

1 Exchanging
Do several examples like this:

Count out twenty-seven units. Exchange them for tens.

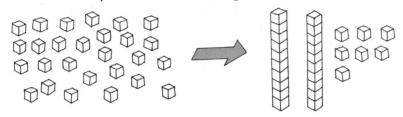

Write   twenty-seven = 27 = 2 tens and 7 units

2 Exchanging game
Each child throws a dice which gives his/her score for that round and collects the appropriate number of units. Whenever ten units are accumulated these are exchanged for one ten.

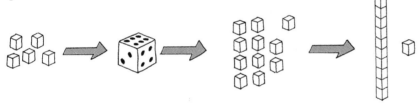

original score is 5   6 more is scored   exchange for 1 ten   new score is 11

The first person to reach 50 (5 tens) or more wins the game.

3 Representing numbers
■ Hold up a flashcard, for example, 37.

Ask the children to put out material to represent this number.

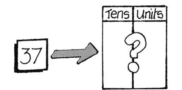

■ Put out, for example, 4 tens and 5 units. Ask 'What number is this?'

Tens	Units

The children then write 4 tens and 5 units = 45.

Workbook 1 Page 19   *Introducing structured material*

The illustration at the top of Page 19 is drawn to full size so that the children may place one ten and four units over the pictured material. Questions 1 and 2 involve putting out tens and units and recording the number this represents, for example, 3 tens and 6 units = 30 + 6 = 36. The teacher should discuss the format used in Question 1 beforehand, so that the children are familiar with it for Question 2.

Questions 3 and 4 involve exchanging units for tens until there are fewer than 10 units left. The size of the numbers has been limited to avoid too many exchanges.

APPROXIMATION TO THE NEAREST TEN
Introductory activities

This is a new concept for the children and the language used is important. A number, for example 18, may be said to be 'near to', 'almost' or 'just under' 20. A number such as 22 would be described as 'near to', 'just over' or 'just more than' 20. 'About' 20 could be used in either case.

1   Using a number line

A number line should be used to show a number as being nearer to one ten than another.

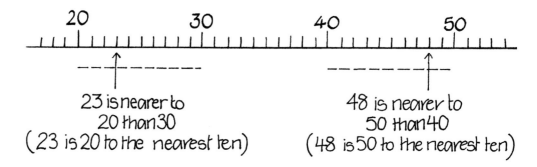

23 is nearer to
20 than 30
(23 is 20 to the nearest ten)

48 is nearer to
50 than 40
(48 is 50 to the nearest ten)

2   Trains

The train scenario used in Workbook 1, Page 20 could be used with 10 chairs in each carriage as shown.

17 people on the train

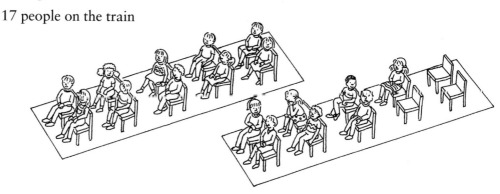

1 full carriage of ten and 1 carriage with more seats occupied than empty.
17 is 20 to the nearest ten.

Workbook 1 Page 20 *Approximation to the nearest ten*

Page 20 introduces the Adventure World theme, details of which were given on Page 43. The queue scenario could be used for some of the examples in Question 1, each of which involves 'rounding down'. The expression, 'to the nearest ten' is used consistently for all examples on the page, but teachers might wish to mention other forms of expression, as indicated in the preceding notes.

Examples in Question 2 involve 'rounding up', while Question 3 has a mixture of 'rounding up' and 'rounding down' to the nearest ten. Examples with 5 units are not used.

ADDITION OF TENS AND UNITS

The emphasis is on the development of a written technique for addition of tens and units using the following approach

- the children use structured material to find an answer which is then recorded. This is accompanied by the appropriate language.

- the teacher shows how the written technique evolves from the use of materials.

- the children practise the written technique using materials only if necessary.

Mental methods and the use of a calculator are also encouraged. The method to be used, mental, written algorithm, or calculator, will depend on the complexity of the addition and the ability of the child.

ADDING UNITS TO TENS AND UNITS: NO CARRYING
Introductory activities

· Ma 3/3a 2/2ab 2/3a
AS/B1,2 RTN/B1 PS/B2

The following activities make use of a number line and also tens and units material.

1 Patterns on a number line

Use a number line to show how a basic addition fact such as 4 + 2 = 6 is related to 14 + 2 = 16, 24 + 2 = 26 and so on.

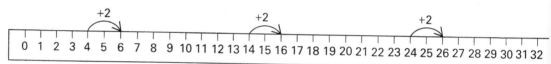

4 + 2 = 6   14 + 2 = 16   24 + 2 = 26

This activity can be related to the scenario at the top of Workbook 1, Page 21, where the number line is represented by a Big Dipper.

It is useful to write the pattern vertically and to emphasise the language.

> 4 + 2 = 6   four add two is six

14 + 2 = 16   fourteen add two is sixteen
24 + 2 = 26   twenty-four add two is twenty-six
34 + 2 = 36   thirty-four add two is thirty-six

In this way a more difficult addition, for example 64 + 2, can be related to the basic fact, 4 + 2 and the answer found mentally.

2 Using structured material

Introduce the use of material using a problem relating to Adventure World, for example,

'Thirty-two children and five teachers visit Adventure World. How many people are there altogether?'.

Establish that the addition is
$$\begin{array}{r} 32 \\ + 5 \\ \hline \\ \hline \end{array}$$

Put out 3 tens and 2 units to represent the children.

Put out 5 units to represent the teachers below the 3 tens and 2 units.

Add the units.   Record the answer.

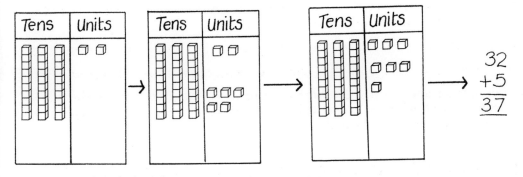

$$\begin{array}{r} 32 \\ +5 \\ \hline 37 \end{array}$$

Because of the simplicity of the examples many children might be able to progress quickly to a written technique without the use of materials.

Workbook 1 Page 21   *Adding units to tens and units: no carrying*

Questions 1 and 2 relate to the Big Dipper number line. All questions could be done by using the number line and counting on. The resulting pattern would help to establish how a more difficult addition such as 45 + 3 could be related to the basic fact 5 + 3.

Question 3 uses vertical setting. Some children may still require structured material for these examples. Care should be taken with examples involving zero.

It is hoped that the children might do the examples in Question 4 by using the thought process shown.

ADDING UNITS TO TENS AND UNITS: WITH CARRYING
Introductory activities

1   Patterns on a number line

Use a number line to show how a basic addition fact, for example, 7 + 5 = 12 is related to other additions such as 17 + 5 = 22, 27 + 5 = 32, and so on.

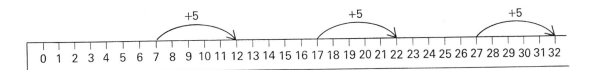

7 + 5 = 12   17 + 5 = 22   27 + 5 = 32

This could be related to the scenario at the top of Workbook 1, Page 22. As before the pattern should be written vertically in the hope that some children will see how a more difficult addition can be related to a basic fact and the answer found mentally.

2 Using structured materials

Set the scene using a problem such as

'In the queue for the Big Dipper there were 35 children and 8 adults. How many people were there altogether?'

Establish that the addition is   35
                                  + 8
                                  ‾‾‾

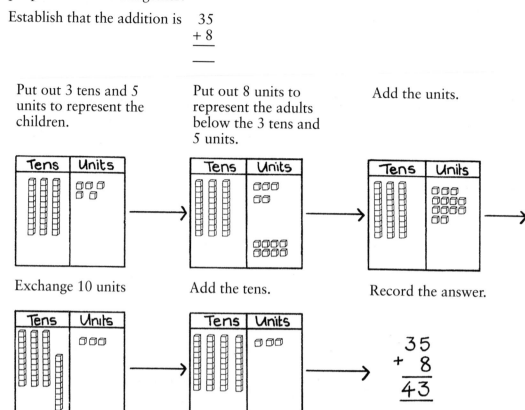

Put out 3 tens and 5 units to represent the children.

Put out 8 units to represent the adults below the 3 tens and 5 units.

Add the units.

Exchange 10 units

Add the tens.

Record the answer.

$$\begin{array}{r} 35 \\ +\ 8 \\ \hline 43 \end{array}$$

The children should do several examples in this way.

3 Introducing a written technique

Once the method of finding the answer using structured material has been established the written technique should be introduced. This technique relates closely to the use of structured material. The precise wording used when carrying out the process will depend on the teacher. One possible wording is as follows

$$\begin{array}{r} 35 \\ +\ 8 \\ \hline \\ \hline \end{array}$$ '35 add 8.

$$\begin{array}{r} 35 \\ +\ 8 \\ \hline 3 \\ \hline 1 \end{array}$$ Add the units. 8 units and 5 units give 13 units.
Exchange 10 units for 1 ten.
Write the 3 in the units column of the answer and carry the 1 ten as shown.

$$\begin{array}{r} 35 \\ +\ 8 \\ \hline 43 \\ \hline 1 \end{array}$$ Add the tens.
1 ten and 3 tens gives 4 tens.
Write the 4 in the tens column of the answer.
The answer is 43.'

Questions 1 and 2 differ from the equivalent questions on Workbook 1, Page 21 in that the first example in each sequence is not a basic number fact. All answers can be found using the Big Dipper number line. Children should be encouraged to find the answers in Question 4 mentally by using the thought processes shown.

ADDING TENS AND UNITS TO TENS AND UNITS: NO CARRYING
Introductory activities

1 Using structured materials

Set the scene using a problem such as

'32 people are on a train. Another 14 people get on. How many people are on the train now?'

Establish that the addition is

$$\begin{array}{r} 32 \\ +14 \\ \hline \end{array}$$

| Put out 3 tens and 2 units. | Put out 1 ten and 4 units below the 3 tens and 2 units. | Add the units and add the tens. | Record the answer. |

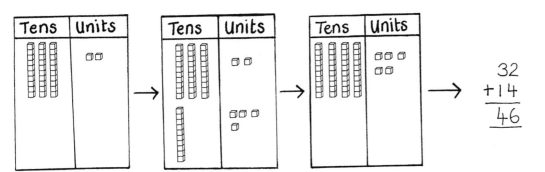

Because of the simplicity of the examples, the children should soon be able to do examples of this type without the use of materials.

$$\begin{array}{r} 32 \\ +14 \\ \hline 6 \end{array}$$ 'Add the units.

$$\begin{array}{r} 32 \\ +14 \\ \hline 46 \end{array}$$ Now add the tens.

46 The answer is 46.'

The children should be encouraged to add the units first when using the written algorithm.

2 Mental additions

At this stage few children will be able to add two two-digit numbers mentally, for example, 32 + 14. However some children should be given practice in adding 10 or even 20 or 30 to a two-digit number mentally. The thought process for adding 46 and 10 might be '*forty*-six and another ten is *fifty*-six.'

Workbook 1 Page 23 *Adding tens and units: no carrying*

The scenario is that of the Adventure World train. Questions 1 and 2 give practice in simple two-digit additions.

Question 3 gives practice in adding on ten to a two-digit number. The children should see the pattern of the tens digit increasing by one each time.

ADDING TENS AND UNITS TO TENS AND UNITS: WITH CARRYING
Introductory activities

1   Using structured materials

Set the scene using a problem such as

'Kim had two rides on the Go-Karts. She did 28 laps and then another 19. How many laps did she do altogether?'

Establish that the addition is

$$28 \\ + 19$$

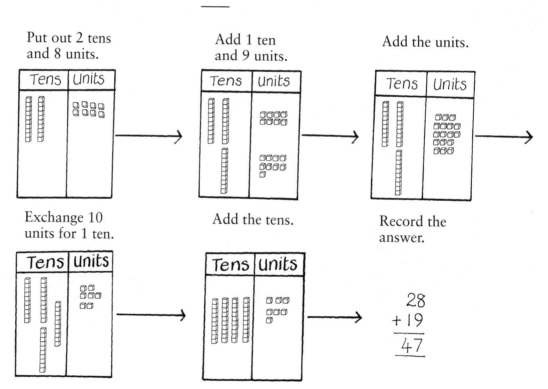

Put out 2 tens and 8 units.

Add 1 ten and 9 units.

Add the units.

Exchange 10 units for 1 ten.

Add the tens.

Record the answer.

$$28 \\ + 19 \\ \hline 47$$

The children should do several examples like this.

2   The written technique

The above process should be practised before dispensing with the use of materials and moving to the written technique.

$$28 \\ + 19$$

'28 add 19'

```
  28      Add the units. 9 units and 8 units gives 17 units.
+ 19      Exchange 10 units for 1 ten.
 ─────    Write the 7 in the units column of the answer and 'carry' the 1 ten.
   7
  1
```

```
  28      Add the tens. 1 ten and 1 ten gives 2 tens and another 2 tens gives 4
+ 19      tens.
 ─────    Write the 4 in the tens column of the answer.
  47      The answer is 'forty-seven.'
  1
```

Ma 2/2a 2/3a 1/3d
AS/B2

Workbook 1 Page 24   *Adding tens and units: with carrying*

Questions 1 to 4 give practice in two-digit additions with carrying. The examples relate to Go-Karts and Golf at Adventure World.

In Question 5 the children may need to do several additions before finding two numbers which add to 50. A calculator may be used. Notes on the use of a calculator are given on Page 32.

ADDING THREE SINGLE-DIGIT NUMBERS: ASSOCIATIVE LAW   Introductory activities

Ma 2/3a 2/2a 1/3d
AS/B1

These activities should make the children aware of the associative nature of addition, that is, when adding more than two numbers, the final answer is the same regardless of the order in which the numbers are added. The activities also help children realise that it is sometimes easier to add numbers in a different order to that given, particularly where two of the numbers add to 10 as, for example, in $\overbrace{4+8+6}$.

1   Does order matter?

Discuss with the children how to make up a fruit drink with orange, lime and lemonade. It does not matter in which order the orange, lime or lemonade are mixed, the end result is the same. Ask the children to give other examples where the final result is the same no matter the order in which the activities are carried out.

Discuss the method of adding three numbers. No matter which pair is added first, the answer is the same.

$$\begin{array}{lll} \overbrace{3+4}+5 & 3+\overbrace{4+5} & \overbrace{3+4+5} \\ =7+5 & =3+9 & =8+4 \\ =12 & =12 & =12 \end{array}$$

2   Composition of ten

Some children find the number facts for ten easy to remember and they use pairs of numbers which add to ten when adding lists of numbers. For example, when adding $6+5+4$, a child might find the answer by saying

'6 and 4 gives 10 and 5 gives 15.'

Give children practice in adding sets of numbers, two of which add to 10, for example, $7+4+3$, $7+5+5$ and so on.

Workbook 1 Page 25   *Adding: associative law*

The scenario of Pages 25 and 26 is that of the Driving School in Adventure World. Questions 2 and 3 verify for the children the associative nature of addition. In order to do these questions the children have to be able to add a two-digit and single-digit number mentally.

Magic squares provide the theme for Questions 4 and 5. Explain to the children what is meant by a Magic square, i.e. the totals for each row and column and also along each diagonal are the same. The examples also provide the opportunity for using the number facts for 10 in order to find an answer more quickly.

Workbook 1 Page 26   *Adding: consolidation*

Questions 1 and 2 provide a miscellaneous set of additions of two-digit numbers. In Question 2, the scouts, guides, brownies and cubs fill two of the stands at the Driving School. In Question 3, the total number of brownies and cubs (91) matches the total number of seats in the green stand while in Question 4 the total number of scouts and guides (72) fills the yellow stand.

Question 5 gives practice in adding sets of three numbers, some of them single-digit numbers. Two of the examples have pairs of numbers adding to 10 in the units column.

ADDITION: PROBLEMS, LANGUAGE, CALCULATOR WORK
Introductory activities

1   Language – addition words

It is important that children know a variety of words which imply that an addition has to be performed, for example 'sum', 'total', 'plus'. Other words such as 'and' and 'altogether' can also often indicate an addition. Sometimes one word seems to be more appropriate than another. For example, 'Find the total score.' 'What is the sum of 3 and 8?'

A word bank could be build up of the various words which indicate that you have to add. The children should be encouraged to make up questions using a variety of addition words. Flashcards could be made of the addition words and questions asked such as

'What is 6 | and | 7?'

'What is | the sum of | 6 and 7?'

'What is 6 | plus | 7?'

'What is 6 | added to | 7?'

and so on.

2 Using a calculator

The children should already have used a calculator (see Workbook 1, Page 9 and these Teacher's Notes, Pages 32–33). However, this may be the first time that children use a calculator to add two-digit numbers.

Discuss some examples with the children, for example, 14 + 37.

Enter 14. Press $\boxed{+}$ $\boxed{3}$ $\boxed{7}$ $\boxed{=}$ to give 51

This can be checked by clearing the display and doing the addition again or by reversing the order in which the numbers are entered.

Enter 37. Press $\boxed{+}$ $\boxed{1}$ $\boxed{4}$ $\boxed{=}$ to give 51

It is also important that the children know that during the addition of three or more numbers, intermediate displays are shown and only when the $\boxed{=}$ is pressed is the final total show on the display. For example, 15 + 16 + 17

Enter		
$\boxed{15}$	$\longrightarrow$	15
$\boxed{+}$	$\longrightarrow$	15
$\boxed{16}$	$\longrightarrow$	16
$\boxed{+}$	$\longrightarrow$	31
$\boxed{17}$	$\longrightarrow$	17
$\boxed{=}$	$\longrightarrow$	48

Such an example should be checked by adding the numbers in a different order.

Textbook Pages 6, 7 and 8 *Language of addition, calculator work*

Pages 6, 7 and 8 contain questions which

■ revise the language of addition

■ require the use of a calculator for additions

■ involve problem solving

On Pages 7 and 8 point out the sequence of question numbers which start at the bottom left of Page 7. The children could make use of their answers to Questions 1 and 2 to help find the answer to Question 3, in that each time one number has been added five times.

The answers to Questions 11 and 12 will probably be found by trial and error. The important point in Question 11 is that the digit 5 has to be the tens digit in the two-digit number. In Question 12, children should try to find 21 in as many different ways as they can using any or all of the keys.

Problem solving

Ma 2/2ab 2/3a
M/B1 AS/B2

Money to 49p, involving 1p, 2p, 5p, 10p and 20p coins was introduced in Workbook 3 of Heinemann Mathematics 2 and is now revised.

The Adventure World theme is continued with the children visiting the Kiosk.

1 Pocket money

Children could be given pocket money to spend at the Kiosk and asked to count how much they have been given. Real or plastic coins could be used, together with purses, bags, tins, etc.

- Show the children how to arrange the coins in order, largest values first, to help them to count, like this:

'ten. . .   twenty . . .   thirty . . .   thirty-five . . .   thirty-seven . . .   thirty-eight'

Repeat for other amounts up to 49p, and also include the 20p coin.

- Give each child in the group a purse or bag containing coins to count. Ask

'Who has the most money?'

'Who has the least money?'

'Who has more than 40p?' and so on.

2 Coin cards

As an alternative to purses, coin cards with divisions for different coins could be used.

- On a card put out coins for the children to count.

Show the children how to rearrange the coins starting with the 20p then 10p

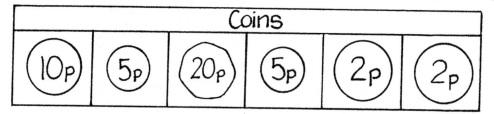

coins.

Help them to count like this:

'twenty . . .   thirty . . .   thirty-five . . .   forty . . .   forty-two . . .   forty-four . . .'

- Give each child a blank card to play this game.

  Each child in turn picks a coin from a bag until the coin card contains six coins. The coins are then rearranged and counted. The child with most money wins the game.

- Make a dice with faces marked 20p, 10p, 5p, 2p, 2p, 1p.

  Each child throws the dice, in turn, and places the appropriate coin on the card. The winner is the first player to have more than 45p.

3 Money bag

Challenge the children to 'feel' in a bag containing up to 5 coins and say how much they think is in the bag. The coins are then withdrawn and counted. For some children it may be a sufficient challenge to identify each coin in the bag while the others do the counting.

4 The Kiosk drinks machine

In this activity the children are introduced to putting out coins to match a price.

Ask a child to put coins in a drinks or snacks machine which can be made by using an old box. For example,

  'Buy a drink costing 34p.'

Each coin should be counted as it is inserted. The box should then be opened and the total value of the coins checked.

5 Individual activities

The activities suggested below provide practice in putting out coins for a given total.

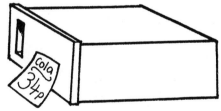

- Bus fare to Adventure World: the child pays the exact fare.

- Kiosk: the child puts out the exact money to buy items which are priced in the Kiosk.

- Adventure World admission prices: the child chooses and pays the exact money.

It is important, also, to encourage the child to lay out sets of different coins which give the same total amount.

    or

Workbook 1 Page 27 *Money to 49p*

In Question 2, the children might lay out different sets of coins to purchase any one item. They should be encouraged, however, to use the least number of coins for any one price, which means using as few boxes as possible on the coin cards.

THE 50P COIN AND MONEY TO 99p
Introductory activities

In this section, the 50p coin is introduced. The emphasis is on counting collections of coins to 99p and laying out coins to match a given value. The Adventure World theme is continued with the children visiting the Swimming Pool.

1 Birthday presents

Show the children that five 10p coins are equivalent to one 50p coin. Establish other equivalences of 50p, for example 20p, 20p and 10p.

Pictures of birthday presents for mum, dad or a friend can be taken from magazines and mounted on card.

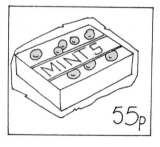  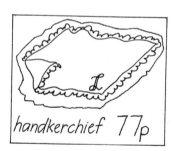

Ask the children to choose one gift and put out coins to pay for it using a 50p coin.

Repeat for other presents and other prices.

2 Collecting for charity

Cans could be filled with coins (maximum value 99p), emptied and the children asked to find the total amounts. The coins should be sorted, ordered, and then counted.

3 Further activities

The activities described on Pages 58–59 for money to 49p could be adapted for amounts to 99p.

For Page 29, Question 2, a different coloured tick could be used for each article. This would make checking easier if a mistake was made.

For Page 30, real, plastic or cardboard coins could be used and sorted so that the totals can be more easily counted. Alternatively, the children could tick each coin as it is counted. They should be encouraged to start counting with the coins of the largest denomination.

MONEY TO 99p
Additional activities

1   Purse cards

Workcards showing purses (or bags) could be made up like the ones shown.

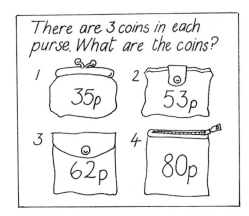

There are 3 coins in each purse. What are the coins?

1 35p   2 53p

3 62p   4 80p

2   Game   *(for 2 to 4 players)*

This game requires a track, as shown, a dice, counters and a box of 5p, 10p, 20p and 50p coins. Each child in turn, throws the dice, and moves his or her counter forward. If the counter lands on a 20p, the player takes a 20p coin from the box. The winner is the first player to collect one of each of the coins 5p, 10p, 20p and 50p.

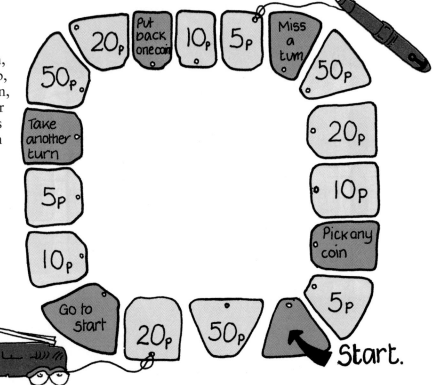

61

Subtracting tens and units
Change from 20p and 50p
Addition and subtraction within 99

Ma 1/3abd
Ma 2/2b
Ma 2/3ae
Ma 3/2ab
Ma 3/3a
RTN/B1
M/B1
AS/B1,2
FE/B1
PS/B2
PSE

Overview

This section

- introduces subtraction of tens and units

- introduces change from 20p and 50p and deals with addition and subtraction of money to 99p

- presents word problems on addition and subtraction of tens and units.

	Teacher's Notes	Workbook 1	Textbook
Subtraction of tens and units	64		
Subtracting units from tens and units Without exchange	64	31	
Subtracting tens and units from ten and units Without exchange	66	32	
Subtracting units from tens and units With exchange	68	33	
Subtracting tens and units from tens and units With exchange	71	34	
Subtraction of tens and units: language, puzzles, calculator work	72		9–12
Money: change from 20p and 50p	74	35, 36	
Money: addition and subtraction to 99p	76	37, 38	
Addition and subtraction within 99			13, 14
Other activities			*15, 16*
Extension			*12*
Problem solving		*38*	*10, 12, 15*

Key words and phrases

subtract	dearest	How many left?	odd number
minus	cheapest	Count out the change	even number
less than	change	Use tens and units if you wish	
difference between		Exchange	

Resources

Useful materials

- Tillich or Dienes base 10 material
- number lines (1 to 50)
- 1p, 2p, 5p, 10p, 20p and 50p coins
- other materials suggested within the introductory activities
- flashcards of key words and phrases

Assessment and Resources Pack

Assessment

Check-ups

Check-up 5
Workbook 1 Pages 31–34
(Subtraction from TU)

Check-up 6
Workbook 1 Pages 35–38
(Money: change from 20p, 50p
+ and – to 99p)

Check-up 7
Workbook 1 Pages 1–38
(+ and –, tens and units)

Assessment in Context

Assessment in Context 1
The bus journey

Assessment in Context 2
Playtime

Resources

Problem Solving Activities

Calculator puzzle
6 (Subtraction of tens and units)

Resource Cards

Resource Cards 10 and *11* (What's the
difference?) involve subtraction of tens
and units.

Resource Cards 12 and *13* (Adventure
Trail) involve mental addition and
subtraction (TU ± U).

Teaching notes

SUBTRACTION OF TENS AND UNITS

The initial approach suggested is to use number lines and pattern, where a basic fact such as 5 − 3 is related to 15 − 3, 25 − 3, etc. Tens and units material is then used to establish a written technique. For more difficult examples decomposition, involving exchanging a ten for ten units, is the method outlined in these notes. Alternatively, a technique other than decomposition could be used as the examples in Workbook 1, Pages 31 to 34 do not depend on a specific method. Where appropriate, there is an emphasis on mental subtraction.

The Adventure World theme is continued here by using scenarios involving the Swimming Pool and an Adventure Trail.

SUBTRACTING UNITS FROM TENS AND UNITS WITHOUT EXCHANGE
Introductory activities

Ma 2/3a 3/3a
AS/B1,2 RTN/B1 PS/B2

The activities given below involve subtraction patterns illustrated on a number line, and the use of tens and units material. There is also an emphasis on mental subtraction by relating an example such as 47 − 3 to the basic subtraction fact 7 − 3 which the child already knows.

1   Patterns on a number line

■ Use a number line to illustrate a basic subtraction fact which the children know, such as 5 − 3. Place a counter on 5 and jump back 3.

5 − 3 = 2

Children at this stage can accept a 'jump back' on a number line as equivalent to taking away.

■ Do the same for other subtractions related to the basic fact 5 − 3.

5 − 3 = 2   15 − 3 = 12   25 − 3 = 22

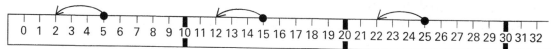

Emphasise the pattern:

'5 take away 3 is 2.'
'25 take away 3 is 22.'

Repeat for other basic facts where the children place counters and count back. For example,

7 − 2 = 5   17 − 2 = 15   27 − 2 = 25   37 − 2 = 35

■ This activity could be related to the scenario at the top of Workbook 1, Page 31 where the number line represents the length, in metres, of the Swimming Pool. Aziz is 8 metres from the end of the pool. He swims another 5 metres. How many metres has he left to swim? 8 − 5 = 3, etc.

2 Using tens and units

This activity could be related to the Swimming Pool theme in Question 3 on Page 31 of Workbook 1. A drawing or a piece of blue paper might be used to represent the pool. The number of children in the pool, for example 39, should be represented by tens and units placed on a notation card.

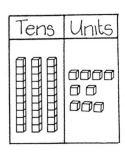

'4 children leave the pool to get changed.'

Write   39
          − 4
          ———

Remove 4 cubes.
'9 units take away 4 units leaves 5 units. There are 35 left in the pool.'

Write   39
          − 4
          ———
           35

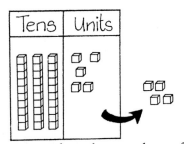

Repeat for other numbers of children leaving the pool.

■ Change the number of children in the pool and repeat the above activity. Make sure that the subtraction does not involve exchanging at this stage.

■ Some children could be led to predict the answer before removing cubes as they see the relationship with a basic subtraction fact. For example, they may realise 39 − 2 is 37 because 9 − 2 is 7 and then use material to confirm the result.

3 Mental subtraction

The following activities may help the children to calculate mentally.

■ Use cards with a basic subtraction fact on one side and a related, more difficult subtraction on the other. For example,

| 6−4 | The children should provide the answer 2.

Turn over | 86−4 | 'What is 86 take away 4?'

A number line could be used to check by counting back.

■ Use a card such as | 56 | . Cover up the 5 tens. | 6 | .

'What is 6 − 2?'   Then uncover the 5 and ask 'what will 56 − 2 be?'

- Use tens and units material. Put out 6 units. Ask the children to predict how many units are left if 4 are taken away. (Do not remove the 4 cubes.)

Now add tens to the 6 units and ask them to subtract 4 mentally each time and predict the answer.

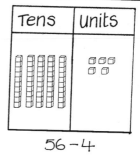

Tens	Units

36 – 4   26 – 4   56 – 4

Ma 2/3a 3/3a
AS/B1,2 PS/B2

Workbook 1 Page 31   *Subtracting units from tens and units*

The top half of Page 31 depends on the use of a number line to investigate patterns as suggested in the introductory activities. All of the examples could be done by counting back using the number line given at the top of the page. In Question 2 discuss the completed patterns with the children. '8 take away 6 is 2', '18 take away 6 is 12', '28 take away 6 is 22', 'What would 38 take away 6 be?'

Question 3 introduces vertical setting and the use of tens and units material for pupils who require this. The examples in Question 4 could also be done using materials although, as the cartoon suggests, it is hoped that some children would be able to do them mentally by, for example, relating 27 – 4 to 7 – 4.

SUBTRACTING TENS AND UNITS FROM TENS AND UNITS WITHOUT EXCHANGE
Introductory activities

Ma 2/3a
AS/B2 RTN/B1

1   Using tens and units

The Swimming Pool theme might be used again to link with the examples on Page 32 of Workbook 1.

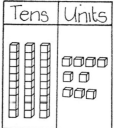

'39 children in the pool.

14 children go to the showers.'

Write   39
          – 14
          ____

'39 take away 14.

Subtract the units. 9 units take away 4 units is 5 units.

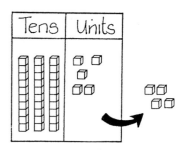

66

Subtract the tens. 3 tens take away 1 ten is 2 tens.

There are 25 children left in the pool.'

Write
$$\begin{array}{r} 39 \\ -\,14 \\ \hline 25 \end{array}$$

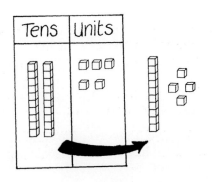

Repeat for other numbers of children in the pool and going to the showers.

2 How many more?

Add a 'small pool' to the one used in Activity 1. This scenario is used at the foot of Workbook 1, Page 32.

Discuss the question 'How many more children are in the big pool than in the small one?' The children have previously met the language 'how many more' and should realise that the answer is found by subtraction.

Write
$$\begin{array}{r} 39 \\ -\,14 \\ \hline \\ \hline \end{array}$$

The children could then use the tens and units materials to find an answer in the same way as outlined in Activity 1.

3 A written technique

At first the children should use tens and units materials to find answers which are then written down after looking at the material to see what is left. Give enough time to establish this process before moving to a written method. The written technique should match as closely as possible what happens when materials are used. It is most important to take enough time to establish this link between use of concrete materials and a written algorithm.

The wording given below is not the only possible version. Choose your own wording to match the use of materials and the language used in your school.

$$\begin{array}{r} 86 \\ -\,23 \\ \hline \\ \hline \end{array}$$ '86 take away 23.

$$\begin{array}{r} 86 \\ -\,23 \\ \hline 3 \\ \hline \end{array}$$ Subtract the units.
6 take away 3 is 3.

$$\begin{array}{r} 86 \\ -\,23 \\ \hline 63 \end{array}$$ Subtract the tens.
8 take away 2 is 6.
The answer is 63.'

Workbook 1 Page 32 *Subtracting tens and units from tens and units*

Question 2 will require explanation as the numbers in the speech bubbles indicate the number of lengths each boy has swum. Some children may be able to predict which boy has the smallest number of lengths still to swim before doing the subtractions.

Question 3 involves the comparison aspect of subtraction. Encourage the children to put their answers into words – 'There are 53 more children in the big pool'.

SUBTRACTING UNITS FROM TENS AND UNITS WITH EXCHANGE
Introducing activities

The activities below make use of the Adventure Trail scenario from Workbook 1. There are many other ways of introducing the decomposition method of subtraction.

1 Revision of subtraction facts

Subtraction facts of the type $15 - 8 = 7$, $13 - 6 = 7$, $17 - 9 = 8$ are required for

subtractions such as $\begin{array}{r} 65 \\ -\ 8 \\ \hline \end{array}$ $\begin{array}{r} 43 \\ -\ 6 \\ \hline \end{array}$ $\begin{array}{r} 57 \\ -\ 9 \\ \hline \end{array}$ which appear in Activity 2.

Such facts should be revised.

One way of doing this is to introduce the idea of the Adventure Trail which is used on Pages 33 and 34 of Workbook 1. The Adventure Trail is a path which goes through the woods and crosses a river. There are things to do, to climb, and to jump over. In doing so points are scored and penalty points are lost. For example,

'Jackie has 17 points and loses 9 penalty points. How many has she left?'

2 Patterns on a number line

Use a number line to discuss subtractions related to basic subtraction facts such as $13 - 6$. Answers are found by counting back.

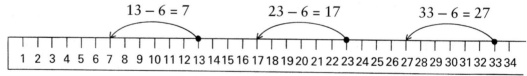

$$13 - 6 = 7 \qquad 23 - 6 = 17 \qquad 33 - 6 = 27$$

Repeat for other basic facts.

Some children may be able to count back in their heads or make use of a basic fact to arrive at an answer mentally.

This activity is related to the first part of Page 33 of Workbook 1, which introduces the Adventure Trail and could be used at this point.

One way of introducing the Trail is to use a long strip of wallpaper as a 'bridge' with numbered rungs. Ask a child to stand on one of the numbered lines and then move back. There is a bridge like this on Workbook 1, Page 33.

$34 - 6$

3 Using tens and units involving exchange

The children have already exchanged 10 units for 1 ten when adding. They should now practise exchanging in the reverse direction, from 1 ten to 10 units. This is to prepare for the introduction of the decomposition method of subtraction. Discuss with them examples like the following:

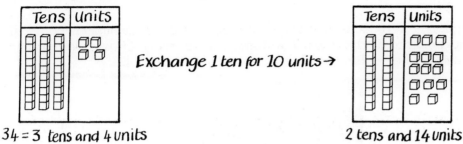

This could be recorded as

34 → 3 tens and 4 units → 2 tens and 14 units.

It is also worthwhile showing the exchange as $^2\cancel{3}\,^14$.

Ask the children to do further examples like this where they exchange 1 ten for 10 units.

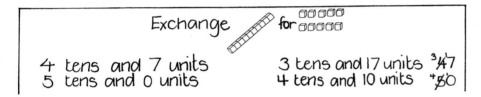

4 Introducing decomposition

Introduce the decomposition method for subtractions such as 45 − 8 by using structured tens and units material. The idea of penalty points might be continued, for example, by starting with 45 points and asking one of the children to choose a single-digit card from a box to give the penalty. The penalty should always require a decomposition to be performed.

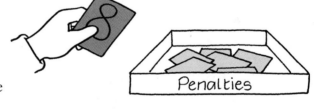

'45 take away 8. Subtract the units. 5 units take away 8 units.

There are not enough units.'

Ask the children where more units could be found.

'Exchange 1 ten for 10 units.

Now there are 3 tens and 15 units.

15 units take away 8 units leaves 7 units.

The answer is 37 points.'

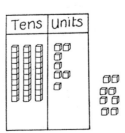

The numbers of starting points and penalty points could be varied to give further practice.

69

5 A written technique

At this stage the children should use structured material to model the subtraction process and then write down the final answer by looking at the material which is left. Time should be given for this process to become established before introducing a written algorithm which should be very closely linked to the use of the concrete materials.

Examples for introducing and practising a written technique might continue the penalty points idea. One possible wording is given below. Choose wording to suit your class and the subtraction language used in your school.

Score	52
Penalty	7
New score	?

$$\begin{array}{r} 52 \\ -\ 7 \\ \hline \end{array}$$
'52 take away 7.

$$\begin{array}{r} {}^{4}\cancel{5}\ {}^{1}2 \\ -\ 7 \\ \hline \end{array}$$
Subtract the units. 2 take away 7   I cannot.
Exchange 1 ten for 10 units. I now have 4 tens and 12 units.

$$\begin{array}{r} {}^{4}\cancel{5}\ {}^{1}2 \\ -\ 7 \\ \hline 5 \end{array}$$
12 take away 7 leaves 5.

$$\begin{array}{r} {}^{4}\cancel{5}\ {}^{1}2 \\ -\ 7 \\ \hline 45 \end{array}$$
There are 4 tens left.
The answer is 45.
The new score is 45 points.'

To summarise, the progression to using a written technique should be as follows:

(i)   use of structured material
(ii) use of material and recording in symbols by referring to the material
(iii) a written technique (but thinking in terms of the material)

Ma 2/3a 3/3a
AS/B1,2 PS/B2

Workbook 1 Page 33   *Subtracting units from tens and units with exchange*

The 'bridge' at the top of Page 33 could be introduced in the way suggested in Introductory Activity 2 on Page 68. It could be used by the children to count back.

In Questions 1 and 2, some children may be able to use a basic fact and the pattern to calculate mentally other examples in the sequence.

Children may need to use tens and units material for the examples in Questions 3 and 4 .

SUBTRACTING TU FROM TU WITH EXCHANGE
Introductory Activities

1 Comparing scores

Give a group of the children photographs, magazine cut-outs or simple cartoons of children who have taken part in the Adventure Trail.

Sara
52 Points

Alan
45 Points

Peter
17 Points

Louise
28 Points

The pictures provide a context for subtraction examples by asking questions such as

'How many more points does Alan have than Louise?'

Discussion should lead to the need to solve the subtraction example

$$\begin{array}{r} 45 \\ -\,28 \\ \hline \end{array}$$

At first, such problems might be solved by subtracting using tens and units material as described below.

2 Using tens and units

The process of decomposition described on Page 69 could be extended for subtracting tens as well as units. For example,

$$\begin{array}{r} 45 \\ -\,28 \\ \hline \end{array}$$

'45 take away 28.

Subtract the units. 5 units take away 8 units
I cannot.

Tens	Units

Exchange 1 ten for 10 units.

I now have 3 tens and 15 units.

Tens	Units

Subtract the units.

15 units take away 8 units leaves 7 units.'

Tens	Units

Subtract the tens.

3 tens take away 2 tens leaves 1 ten.

The answer is 17.'

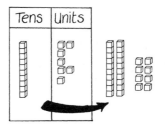

This technique should be firmly established before a written algorithm is introduced. Even then, material should still be available to the children.

3 A written technique

This could now be extended to involve tens as well as units.
For example,

$$\begin{array}{r} 52 \\ -17 \\ \hline \end{array}$$ 'Subtract the units.

2 take away 7   I cannot.

$$\begin{array}{r} {}^{4}\cancel{5}\,{}^{1}2 \\ -1\;7 \\ \hline 5 \end{array}$$ Exchange 1 ten for 10 units
12 take away 7 is 5.

$$\begin{array}{r} {}^{4}\cancel{5}\,{}^{1}2 \\ -\;1\;7 \\ \hline 35 \end{array}$$ Subtract the tens
4 take away 1 is 3
The answer is 35.'

You should alter the details of the wording used to suit your class and the policy of your school. Methods other than decomposition could be used although they may not be so readily explained to young children using structured materials. The workbook examples could be done by children who do not use decomposition but use one of the other methods such as 'Equal Additions' or 'Complementary Addition'.

Ma 2/3a 2/2b
AS/B2

Workbook 1 Page 34   *Subtracting tens and units with exchange*

Page 34 provides practice examples involving exchange.

Questions 2, 3 and 4 use the context of comparing points scored. This is related to Introductory Activity 1 on Page 71.

SUBTRACTION OF TENS AND UNITS: LANGUAGE, PUZZLES, CALCULATOR WORK
Introductory activities

Ma 1/3b 2/3a
AS/B1 PS/B2

Textbook Pages 9 to 12 provide further practice in subtracting tens and units with an emphasis on language, puzzles and calculator work.

1   Language – subtraction words

■ Use a series of cards with the subtraction words and phrases from the top of Textbook Page 9.

| take away | subtract | difference between | minus |

Use the cards to create sentences such as

30 | subtract | 10 gives

where the children supply the answer 20. Show that this can be written in the form 30 − 10 = 20.

Repeat for the other phrases. In the case of 'difference between' discuss at least one example where the smaller number comes first. For example,

The | difference between | 10 and 50 is 40.

It is important to point out the order in which the symbolic form is written:

50 − 10 = 40

■ Children often find this reverse process more difficult, where they start with a statement like

47 − 5 = 42

and have to turn it into a sentence using one of the phrases, for example,

47 | subtract | 5 gives 42

They then have to make up a story about the subtraction, for example,

'I had 47 stickers. I gave 5 away and have 42 left.'

2 Subtraction paths

Textbook Page 10 deals with finding paths where the same number is subtracted each time. Prepare for this by

■ creating paths, for example,

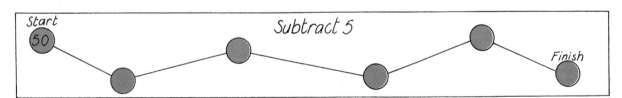

The children should give the numbers for the stepping stones on the path, i.e. 45, 40, 35, 30, 25.

Repeat this activity for other numbers.

■ spotting paths, for example,

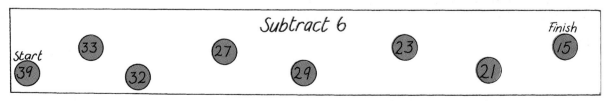

The children should subtract 6 and draw lines to show the correct path.

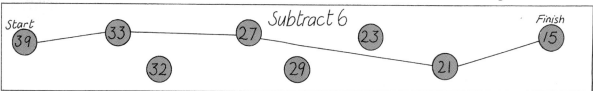

Repeat this activity for other numbers.

Ma 1/3ab 2/2b 2/3a
AS/B2 PS/B2 PSE

Textbook Pages 9 and 10   *Language, subtraction within 99*

The introductory activities indicated previously should help children with the work in Question 1 on each of these pages.

On Textbook Page 9, Questions 1(d), 3(b) and 4(b) are likely to cause difficulty as the two numbers in the subtraction appear in the 'wrong' order.

Problem solving

On Textbook Page 10 the children might enjoy creating further paths of their own. The problem solving activities in Questions 2(b) and 2(c) can be tackled in a number of ways. Some children may subtract 7 from some of the numbers to find a pair with a difference of 7. Others may spot a likely pair and do a mental subtraction to check. Others might add on 7 to some of the smaller numbers. Mental subtraction should be encouraged.

Ma 3/3a 3/2b 1/3ab 2/3a
AS/B2 PS/B2 PSE

Textbook Pages 11 and 12   *Subtraction within 99, calculator work*

Question 1 on Page 11 deals with a pattern where the first number and the answer increase by 10 each time.

Questions 2 to 4 provide work on finding the difference between pairs of numbers. The numbers are made from the digits 1 to 8.

Problem solving

Extension

The extension work on Page 12 is relatively difficult and so the use of a calculator is suggested to allow the children to concentrate on the problem solving aspects. In Question 1, the children might use 'trial and error' to find the answers 10 and 77 in the grids shown.

36	14	
22	(10)	12

(77)	67	10
38	11	

Question 2(c) is more demanding than Questions 2(a) and 2(b).

MONEY: CHANGE FROM 20p AND 50p
Introductory activities

Ma 2/2b 2/3a 1/3b
M/B1 AS/B1

Change from 10p was introduced in Heinemann Mathematics 2. In this section the children use coins to give change from 20p and 50p. They do this by counting on and then checking by subtraction. Checking is important even when change is given automatically by a machine.

The Adventure World context is continued on Workbook 1, Pages 35 and 36 with children spending money in the Gift Shop.

1   Money words

Ask groups of children to list 'money words'. When the groups report back write the words individually on flashcards. Activities could be carried out using the cards, for example,

- reading each word

- using the word in a sentence

- suggesting another word or phrase which means the same

2   The tuck shop   *(change from 10p)*

Revision of giving change from 10p using 1p, 2p, and 5p coins could be carried out using a tuck shop situation. A customer is supplied with a 10p coin to buy one biscuit. The shopkeeper should use 1p, 2p and 5p coins to count out the change.

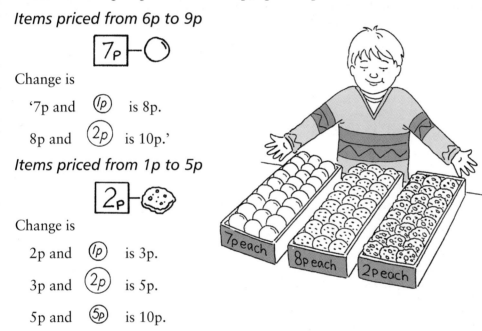

Items priced from 6p to 9p

7p ⊢ ◯

Change is

'7p and (1p) is 8p.

8p and (2p) is 10p.'

Items priced from 1p to 5p

2p ⊢ 🍪

Change is

2p and (1p) is 3p.

3p and (2p) is 5p.

5p and (5p) is 10p.

Children should be encouraged to count on to 5p and then on to 10p.

3   Drinks machine   *(change from 20p)*

Use a large cardboard box with two flaps to simulate a drinks machine to give the children experience of giving change from 20p using 1p, 2p, 5p and 10p coins. The customer puts a 20p coin in the slot and asks for a particular drink. The drink and the change are given by a child who simulates the working of the machine.

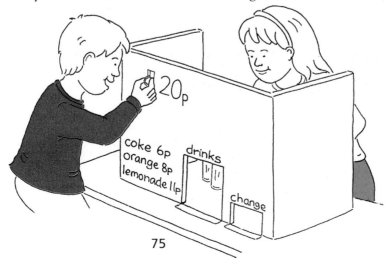

Change is put out for drinks priced:

- from 16p to 19p, using 1p and 2p coins

- from 11p to 15p, using 1p, 2p and 5p coins

    Children should be encouraged to count on to 15p and then to 20p.

- from 6p to 10p, using 1p, 2p and 10p coins

    Children should be encouraged to count on to 10p and then to 20p.

- from 1p to 5p, using 1p, 2p, 5p and 10p coins

    Children should be encouraged to count on to 5p, then to 10p and then to 20p.

4 Newsagents *(change from 50p)*

Set out newspapers and magazines and give each customer a 50p coin to spend. This time change is given using 1p, 2p, 5p, 10p and 20p coins.

For example,

'32p and (1p) is 33p

33p and (2p) is 35p

35p and (5p) is 40p

40p and (10p) is 50p.'

'23p and (2p) is 25p

25p and (5p) is 30p

30p and (20p) is 50p.'

Ma 2/2b 2/3a
M/B1 AS/B1,2

Workbook 1 Pages 35 and 36   *Money: change from 20p, 50p*

On Pages 35 and 36 the children have to:

- lay out coins for change

    This should mirror the work outlined in the introductory activities. Counting on to the intermediate steps of 5p, 10p, 15p, 20p and so on was encouraged so that the children might use as few coins as possible.

- find the total value of coins laid out for the change

- check the change by completing the subtraction

MONEY: ADDITION AND SUBTRACTION TO 99P
Introductory activities

Ma 1/3b 2/2b 2/3a
AS/B2

This section applies addition and subtraction to 99 to money calculations by considering the cost of various events in Adventure World.

1 Tickets

Discuss with the children events in which they might take part during a day visit to Adventure World. Each event could be represented by a ticket showing a price less than 50p (except for swimming which costs 50p).

A child chooses two tickets and could be asked questions such as

'What is the total cost of the two events?'

'What is the difference in price between the two?'

'How much dearer?' . . .

'How much cheaper?' . . .

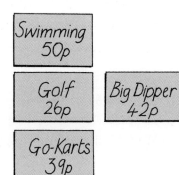

Ma 2/2b 2/3a 1/3ab
AS/B2 PSE

Problem solving

Workbook 1 Page 37 and 38 *Money: addition, subtraction to 99p*

On Page 37, Question 3 the new prices should be found mentally.

These new prices are used on Page 38, where there are white spaces for the children's working.

In Question 5, Taj has to spend 76p on two of the four events shown above in Question 4.

Ma 1/3b 2/3a 3/3a
AS/B2

Textbook Pages 13 and 14 *Addition and subtraction within 99*

On Page 13, discuss the language of each example with the children so that they look for key phrases such as 'how many more', 'total', 'altogether' which give clues about which operation to use.

Questions 3 and 4 depend on the answers to Question 2. These should be checked to avoid a series of errors resulting from a wrong answer in Question 2. In Questions 5 and 6 the children are likely to say that the answers are 'the same'.

On Page 14, Questions 1, 2 and 3 are linked, with each answer depending on the previous one. In Question 5 the children may notice that the answers 9, 7, 5, 3, 1 'go down in twos' or 'you subtract 2 each time' or that they are 'odd numbers'.

Ma 1/3a 2/2b 2/3a
AS/B2 PSE

Problem solving

Textbook Page 15 *Other activity: addition to 99*

■ This number puzzle requires the children to add pairs of two-digit numbers. It could be attempted any time after completion of the addition of tens and units section in Workbook 1.

■ The numeral cards for Questions 1 to 3 can be arranged as shown to give the following totals:

24	25	23	25	23	24	32	42	32	52	42	52
+ 35	+ 34	+ 45	+ 43	+ 54	+ 53	+ 45	+ 35	+ 54	+ 34	+ 53	+ 43
59	59	68	68	77	77	77	77	86	86	95	95

No exchange of units for tens is required in any of these examples.

■ The children could work individually or in pairs. Some discussion of what is required may be necessary. For example

'Put these two cards together side by side.

What number do they make?

Put these two cards below.

What do 52 and 34 add up to

$$\begin{array}{r} \boxed{5}\boxed{2} \\ + \boxed{3}\boxed{4} \\ \hline 8\ 6 \end{array}$$

To find a total of 77, the children are likely to employ a 'guess and check' approach.

Having found, for example, $\begin{array}{r} 23 \\ +\ 54 \\ \hline \end{array}$ as a solution in Question 2(a) some children

may then give $\begin{array}{r} 54 \\ +\ 23 \\ \hline \end{array}$ as their solution in Question 2(b). They should be asked

to find different numbers which add to 77.

Question 3 could be extended to include target totals of 86 and/or 95.

Question 4 is more difficult because for both target totals exchange of units for tens is required. Since card $\boxed{3}$ has to be placed in the position shown, a requirement which may have to pointed out to some children, there are only two solutions for each part of the question.

Additional activity
The following workcard could be provided:

Which of your numbers $\boxed{3}$, $\boxed{4}$, $\boxed{5}$ and $\boxed{6}$ fits each of these additions?

| 1 | $\begin{array}{r} 2\square \\ +\ 34 \\ \hline 5\ 7 \end{array}$ | 2 | $\begin{array}{r} 30 \\ +\ \square 7 \\ \hline 8\ 7 \end{array}$ | 3 | $\begin{array}{r} 3\square \\ +\ 28 \\ \hline 6\ 4 \end{array}$ | 4 | $\begin{array}{r} 26 \\ +\ 5\square \\ \hline 8\ 0 \end{array}$ |

Textbook Page 16   *Other activity: complementary addition*

■ Page 16 could be attempted after completion of the addition of tens and units sections in Workbook1. In that section, basic number facts such as 5 + 3 = 8 and 5 + 7 = 12 were extended to 15 + 3 =   , 25 + 3 =   , 35 + 3 =   and to 45 + 7 =   , 55 + 7 =   , 65 + 7 =   and so on.

■ The work on Page 16 asks questions such as

$$35 + \boxed{} = 42$$

or '35 and what gives 42?'

The children have to guess the answer first. The method used could be

 (i) counting on in ones
 (ii) using trial and error
(iii) recalling the basic number fact (5 + 7 = 12)

The guess is then checked using a calculator.

Some preliminary work might be done, using simple examples such as

$5 + \boxed{} = 9$ $25 + \boxed{} = 29$

'5 and what gives 9?'   '25 and what gives 29?'

$25 + \boxed{} = 30$ $25 + \boxed{} = 33$

'25 and what gives 30?'   '25 and what gives 33?'

79

This workbook is divided into four mathematical sections. Details of the content, resources and language for each section are given at the start of the notes for that section. Each section has its own separate Overview. The four sections are:

	Teacher's Notes
Multiplication: 2, 3, 4, 5, 10 times table	pages 82–107
Division: sharing aspect	pages 108–114
Fractions: halves and quarters	pages 115–119
Division: grouping aspect	pages 120–126

The mathematics in the workbook is set within two contexts:

- *School* where situations and events familiar to children are used to teach and illustrate aspects of the multiplication section.

- *Holiday* where a group of children go camping, visit the beach and the harbour. This context is used in the two division sections and the fraction section.

Workbook 2

Ma 1/3ab
Ma 2/2ab
Ma 2/3abc
Ma 3/2a
Ma 3/3a
Ma 4/1b
RTN/B1
M/B1
AS/B1
MD/B1
PS/B1,2
FE/B1
PM/A1
PSE

Multiplication

Overview

This section

- introduces the concept of multiplication and its associated language and notation
- introduces the 2, 3, 4, 5 and 10 times tables
- introduces the commutative aspect of multiplication
- introduces the £1 coin
- provides practice examples involving word problems including money

	Teacher's Notes	Workbook 2	Textbook
Concept of multiplication	85	1, 2	
Language, notation, and the link with addition	87	3–5	
Concept of multiplication Additional activities	89		
The 2 times table	92	6–8	
The 3 times table	94	9, 10	
Using the 2 and 3 times tables including money	95		17, 18
The 4 times table	96	11, 12	
The 5 times table	97	13, 14	
Using the 4 and 5 times tables including money	98	15, 16	
The 2, 3, 4, 5 times tables Additional activities	99		
The commutative law for multiplication	100	17, 18	
The 10 times table and one hundred	101	19	
The £1 coin	102	20	
Using the 2, 3, 4, 5, and 10 times tables including money	104	21–24	19, 20
Other activity			*21*
Problem solving			*18, 20, 21*
Extension		*8, 10, 22*	*20*

Key words and phrases

Multiplication language such as:
3 sets of 5, 3 times 5, 3 fives, 3 × 5

the same number	find the cost of	How much did you spend?
buy four of each	check	How much change?
one hundred	one pound	total cost

Resources

Useful materials

- sets of objects such as counters, cubes, beads, buttons, model cars, coins, interlocking cubes, books

- sorting boxes, trays and hoops

- coloured pencils

- coloured gummed paper shapes

- calculators

- real, plastic or cardboard coins (10p, 20p, 50p, £1)

- dice

- other materials suggested within the introductory and additional activities

- flashcards of key words and phrases

- multiplication games including computer software

Assessment and Resources Pack

Assessment

Check-ups

Check-up 1
Workbook 2 Pages 1–10
(Concept of multiplication
and 2, 3 times tables)

Check-up 2
Workbook 2 Pages 11–19
(4, 5, 10 times tables)

Check-up 3
Workbook 2 Pages 20–24
(£1 coin and 2, 3, 4, 5 and 10 times tables)

Resources

Problem Solving Activities
7 Donna's dartboard (Multiplication facts)
8 Spinners (Multiplication facts)
9 Coin count (£1 coin)
10 Farm fun (Multiplication facts)

Resource Cards
Resource Cards 14 to 17 (Island hopping) involve multiplication facts.

Resource Cards 18 to 21 (Cash line) involve putting out amounts to £1.

Teaching notes

The context: in school

The work in this multiplication section is set within the context of the school day. Most of the situations and events should be familiar to the children. Some of the situations, for example, the Games Hall, Art time and the Library, form part of the school routine, whilst others, for example Lunchtime, Going home, and Play activities are part of the child's daily routine beyond the classroom.

THE MULTIPLICATION SYMBOL

When children use material to lay out 'bundles of', 'piles of', 'sets of', for example,

they see this as 3 sets of 5 or 3 fives. This is symbolised as '3 × 5' which is read initially as '3 times 5'.

Some teachers write 3 sets with 5 members in each, as '5 × 3' which they read as '5 multiplied by 3'. However, the authors, and others, take the view that for young children, 3 sets of 5 is better symbolised as '3 × 5' rather than '5 × 3' which reverses the factors. Accordingly, all the preliminary practical work and associated language development should support the representation of 3 sets of 5 as 3 fives in the form 3 × 5, read as '3 times five'.

The commutative property of multiplication is introduced in Workbook 2, Page 17, after which '3 × 5' and '5 × 3', for example, are seen to be equivalent. The language 'multiplied by' is omitted until a written technique for multiplication is introduced in Heinemann Mathematics 4.

Ask the children to lay out sets of objects such as counters, cubes, beads, buttons, model cars etc, each set having the same number of members.

1 Equivalent sets

Crayons in trays

'Lay out 4 trays. Put 3 crayons in each.'

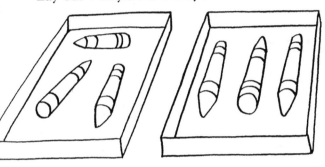
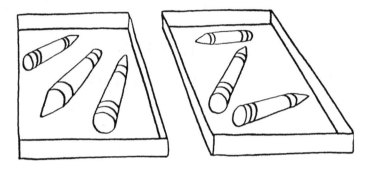

4 sets of 3

A label could then be placed beside the trays as shown.

Repeat this activity for other numbers of trays and crayons.

Different materials may be used:

Apples (plasticine) on paper plates   *Pencils in jars*

3 sets of 5

2 sets of 6

Children in pairs

4 sets of 2

2   Pick a card

Prepare a set of cards, as shown. Ask a child to pick a card:

| 4 sets of 2 | or | 3 sets of 4 | or |

| 2 sets of 6 | or | 4 sets of 3 |

Discuss with the group what to lay out for 4 sets of 2:

'How many sets?' (4)   'Lay out 4 trays.'

'How many crayons in each set?' (2)   'Put 2 crayons in each tray.'

The card picked could then be placed beside the trays.

Repeat this activity for other cards and for different materials.

3   Counting materials

The children should carry out practical activities on their own before they are asked to attempt written work. Provide them with cards, as above, and materials such as cubes, counters, beads, buttons, etc. Ask them to place the objects in sets using sorting boxes, trays, tubs or hoops.

4   Drawings

■ Ask the children to make simple drawings to represent, for example, 3 jars each with 4 lollipops.

3 sets of 4

■ Gummed paper shapes such as stars or triangles could be used.

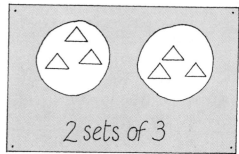

2 sets of 3

Ma 2/3b
MD/B1

Workbook 2 Pages 1 and 2   *Concept of multiplication*

The work on Pages 1 and 2 requires the children to interpret pictures of equivalent sets and complete a recording given in the forms '3 sets of ___', '___ sets of 4' and '___ sets of ___'. It may be necessary to discuss these forms of recording with the children before they begin.

Other ways of expressing and writing, for example, 3 sets of 4, are now introduced, beginning with '3 times 4', '3 fours' and '3 × 4'. Thereafter, the important relationship between multiplication and addition is considered by linking 3 × 4 and 4 + 4 + 4.

1 Introducing 'times' and '×'

Towers of cubes

Ask the children to make 3 towers with 5 cubes in each.

'This is 3 towers of 5, or 3 sets of 5, or 3 fives.'

We say '3 times 5' and write 3 × 5.

Piles of coins

Ask the children to lay out 4 piles with 3 coins in each.

'This is 4 piles of 3, or 4 sets of 3, or 4 threes.'

We say '4 times 3' and write 4 × 3.

Trays of counters

Ask the children to use 2 trays.
Put 6 counters in each.

'This is 2 trays of 6, or
2 sets of 6, or 2 sixes.'

We say '2 times 6' and write 2 × 6.

The children should realise that each of the phrases 'towers of', 'piles of', 'trays of' and 'sets of' can be replaced by 'times' and that this is symbolised by '×'.

2 Using 'times' and '×'

Prepare a variety of labels for the children, for example,

 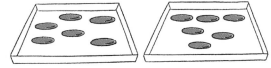

These could be used for the following activities:

Counting materials

Ask the children to select a label and place cubes, counters, beads, etc. appropriately in sorting boxes, trays, tubs and hoops.

Picture cards

A similar activity could be carried out using specially prepared picture cards made by using picture stamps or drawings. Each card should show 1, 2, 3, 4 or 5 pictures of objects and there should be 5 of each making a set of 25 cards. Ask the children to select a label and put out the appropriate picture cards, for example,

Gummed paper shapes

Another version of the picture cards could be made using gummed paper shapes.

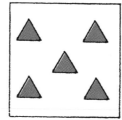  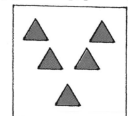

Drawings

Provide simple drawings, or use gummed paper shapes. Ask the children to select an appropriate label. Here are some examples:

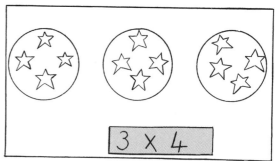

The children could also be asked to select all the appropriate labels, for example,

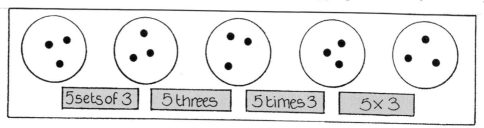

3   The link with addition

After developing the language and notation through activities of the type described above, the children should learn how to find a product using a process of repeated addition.

Counters or interlocking cubes

Ask the children to lay out counters or cubes to show 5×3.

Explain to them that $5 \times 3 = 3 + 3 + 3 + 3 + 3 = 15$.

Similarly, the starting point could be 5 sets of 3 or 5 threes or 5 times 3.

Picture cards

The picture cards described on Page 87 could also be used.
Appropriate cards should be selected, laid out and then a recording made as shown.

$$5 \times 3 = 3 + 3 + 3 + 3 + 3 = 15$$

Drawings

Similar recordings should be made after the children have drawn sets of dots (or made sets using gummed shapes). For example,

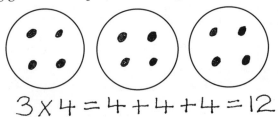

$$3 \times 4 = 4 + 4 + 4 = 12$$

Using a number line

Some children might be made more aware of the link between multiplication and addition by discussion of the situation illustrated, and other similar situations.

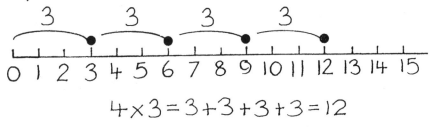

$$4 \times 3 = 3 + 3 + 3 + 3 = 12$$

Workbook 2 Pages 3, 4 and 5   *'Times', '×' and repeated addition*

Provided that the children have been given plenty of practice in the types of introductory activity suggested above they should be able to complete these pages with little further help.

On Page 3 the children are asked to create equivalent sets. This practice should develop their understanding sufficiently for them to interpret the pictures of equivalent sets provided on Page 4.

Ma 2/3ab 1/3b
AS/B1 MD/B1

CONCEPT OF MULTIPLICATION
Additional activities

Many children would benefit from doing extra work on this important topic. Here are suggestions for worksheets and cards which might be used.

Ma 2/3ab
AS/B1 MD/B1

1 Worksheets

Picture stamps, gummed shapes or simple drawings could be used as shown below.

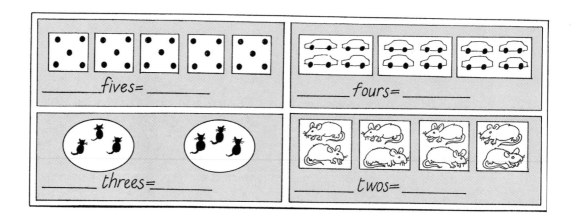

_____ fives = _____   _____ fours = _____

_____ threes = _____   _____ twos = _____

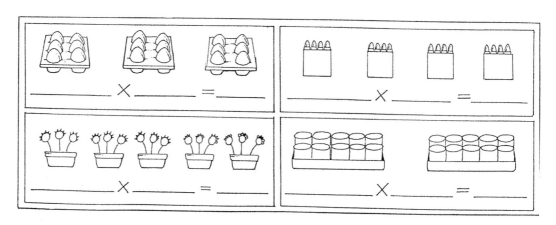

_____ × _____ = _____   _____ × _____ = _____

_____ × _____ = _____   _____ × _____ = _____

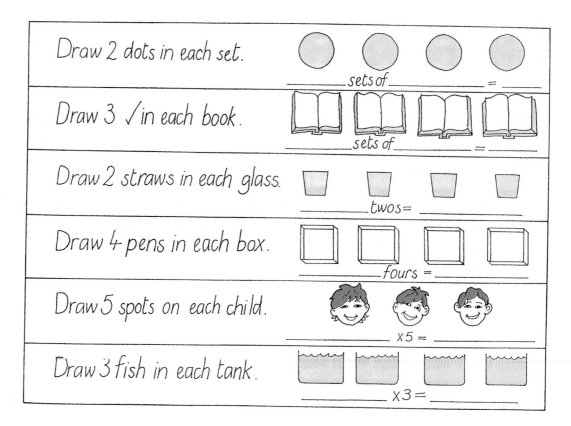

Draw 2 dots in each set.

_____ sets of _____ = _____

Draw 3 ✓ in each book.

_____ sets of _____ = _____

Draw 2 straws in each glass.

_____ twos = _____

Draw 4 pens in each box.

_____ fours = _____

Draw 5 spots on each child.

_____ × 5 = _____

Draw 3 fish in each tank.

_____ × 3 = _____

90

2 Workcards

A selection could be made from the following:

---

1 Use 3 tubs.
Put 4 buttons in each.

Copy and complete

___ sets of ___ = ___

---

2 Use counters.
Put out 5 sets of 3

Copy and complete

___ sets of ___ = ___

---

3 Make 2 strings of
10 beads.

Copy and complete

___ tens = ___

---

4 Make 4 piles of
5 coins.

Copy and complete

___ fives = ___

---

5 Put out cards to
show 5 sets of 3.

Copy and complete

$5 \times 3 =$ ___

---

6 Put out cards to
show 3 sets of 6.

Copy and complete

$3 \times 6 =$ ___

---

7 Lay out counters
to show 3×4.

Draw what you
have put out.

---

8 Use cubes
to show 4×3.

Draw this.

---

9 Draw sets of dots
to show 6×3.

Copy and complete

$6 \times 3 =$ ___

---

10 Draw sets of dots
to show 5×6.

Copy and complete

$5 \times 6 =$ ___

---

11 Draw 3 rings. ◯
Draw 5 marbles
in each.
Copy and complete

$3 \times 5 =$ ___

---

12 Draw 4 jars. ∪
Draw 3 flowers
in each.
Copy and complete

$4 \times 3 =$ ___

91

THE 2, 3, 4, 5, AND 10 TIMES TABLES

■ Each table is built up systematically using materials and/or diagrams, thus reinforcing the concept of multiplication.

■ The 'zero facts', that is 2×0, 3×0, 4×0, 5×0 and 10×0 can be difficult for some children and are not included initially in this build-up. They require a special emphasis and some suggestions for appropriate activities are provided separately on Page 93.

■ The language associated with the tables should be consistent from one teacher to another within a school. For example, the fact $3 \times 6 = 18$ could be stated as '3 times 6 is equal to/equals 18' or '3 times 6 is 18' or '3 sixes are 18'. The phrase 'multiplied by' is omitted until a written technique for multiplication is introduced in Heinemann Mathematics 4.

■ Building up the multiplication tables requires a large amount of oral work and a wide variety of experience. The teacher should provide much more in the way of practice, both oral and written, than can be provided on the workbook and textbook pages. For example, the children should play games, some of which may require the use of a microcomputer or calculator, involving the use of multiplication facts. The aim should be to memorise these facts so that they can be readily recalled.

THE 2 TIMES TABLE
Introductory activities

Ma 2/3ab 3/3a
AS/B1 MD/B1 PS/B2

1 Building up the table

The children could be given a set of interlocking cubes and 2 hoops. The facts and associated language could be built up through teacher-led discussion.

■ 'Put 1 cube in each hoop.
We have 2 ones; that's 2 altogether.
So 2 times 1 equals 2.'

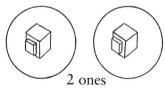

$2 \times 1 = 2$

2 ones

■ 'Put another cube in each hoop. We have 2 twos; that's 4 altogether.
So 2 times 2 equals 4.'

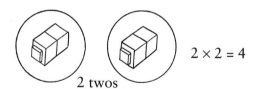

$2 \times 2 = 4$

2 twos

■ 'Put another cube in each hoop', and so on . . .

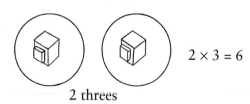

$2 \times 3 = 6$

2 threes

This activity could be repeated using different materials, for example, counters laid out on rectangular sheets of paper, or gummed paper shapes stuck to paper squares.

2 Using the table

Once the table has been built up it could be displayed and used as a basis for oral work. For example,

'2 times 7 is what?'

'2 fives are what?'

'2 times what is 18?'

(The last question could be linked with the recording $2 \times \square = 18$.)

'What is 2 times 5, add 1?'

'2 boxes each hold 6 eggs. How many eggs altogether?'

'1 apple costs 8p. What would 2 apples cost?'

```
2 times table
2 × 1 = 2
2 × 2 = 4
2 × 3 = 6
2 × 4 = 8
2 × 5 = 10
2 × 6 = 12
2 × 7 = 14
2 × 8 = 16
2 × 9 = 18
2 × 10 = 20
```

3 Sequences

Some emphasis should be placed on the sequence, in ascending and in descending order, formed by the 'stations' in the table. Children should be given practice in entering the missing numbers (or stations) in sequences such as 2, 4, 6, 8, $\square$ and 20, 18, 16, 14, $\square$.

More difficult examples could be given, for example, 6, 8, 10, $\square$, $\square$, 16 and 18, 16, 14, $\square$, $\square$, 8.

Children should become aware of the essential feature of the sequence, namely that 2 is being added or subtracted each time.

4 The zero facts

Working with sequences could provide an opportunity to introduce the zero fact, $2 \times 0 = 0$. However, this difficult idea should also be approached in other ways. Use interlocking cubes and hoops as follows:

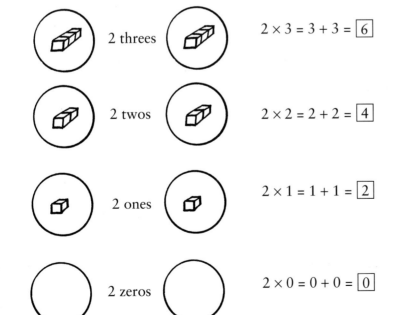

2 threes $2 \times 3 = 3 + 3 = \boxed{6}$

2 twos $2 \times 2 = 2 + 2 = \boxed{4}$

2 ones $2 \times 1 = 1 + 1 = \boxed{2}$

2 zeros $2 \times 0 = 0 + 0 = \boxed{0}$

Workbook 2 Pages 6, 7 and 8 *Building up the 2 times table*

The context for these pages, the School Gym or Games Hall, should be discussed with the children.

For Page 6, Question 1 the children should be made aware that they should use counters to represent sets of children.

A range of language related to the 2 times table is used on Pages 7 and 8. For Page 7, Question 2, the language used in the second part of the question may need to be discussed as, for example, '12 is 2 times 6' is in reverse form to the more familiar '2 times 6 equals 12'.

On Page 8, Question 2, it may help the children if they verbalise examples of the form $2 \times \square = 8$ as '2 times what equals 8?' or '2 whats are 8?'. This is important for the division work in Heinemann Mathematics 4.

On Page 8, Question 4, the children may find it helpful to write the answer for the bracket above the bracket and then complete the addition or subtraction. For example,

$$(2 \overset{16}{\times} 8) + 3 = \square \text{ leading to '16 add 3 is 19'.}$$

Question 5 is for more able children. Nevertheless, writing the answer for the bracket might help. For example $(2 \overset{20}{\times} 10) - \square = 18$, leading to '20 take away what gives 18?'.

THE 3 TIMES TABLE
Introductory activities

While materials should continue to be used in building up the 3 times table, emphasis should now be placed on the repeated addition aspect of multiplication to find products.

The school context is continued by relating the work to equipment used in Art time.

1 Building up the table

Crayons in tubs

■ 'Put 1 crayon in each tub.
We have 3 ones.'

Write $3 \times 1 = 1 + 1 + 1 = 3$

■ 'Put another crayon in each tub.
We have 3 twos.'

Write $3 \times 2 = 2 + 2 + 2 = 6$

Repeat for other numbers of crayons.

Each time encourage the children to find the total number of crayons laid out by adding.

2 Using the table, sequences, zero facts

Work similar to that outlined on Page 93 for the 2 times table, should be done with the 3 times table.

Workbook 2 Pages 9 and 10 *Building up the 3 times table*

The context for these pages, Art time, should be discussed with the children. On Page 9 the children should realise that for 3×5, for example, they are expected to write $3 \times 5 = 5 + 5 + 5 = 15$.

Other activities on Pages 9 and 10 are similar to those for the 2 times table on Pages 6, 7 and 8 and so may pose similar difficulties, particularly Page 10, Questions 5 and 6.

Question 6 is for more able children.

USING THE 2 AND 3 TIMES TABLES INCLUDING MONEY
Introductory activities

Class shop

A section of the class shop could be set up to display articles associated with painting and drawing, for example, crayons, pencils, tubes of paint, paint blocks and chalks. These should be labelled with prices up to 10p. A range of activities might be undertaken:

- Give each child an 'instruction card', for example,

 or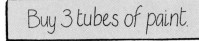

   The customer should work out and tender the correct amount.

- Prepare 'item only' cards, for example,

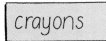

   Allow each child to choose a card and decide whether to buy 2 or 3 of the chosen item.

- Give each child two instruction cards together to make a double purchase.

All of these activities could be extended by requiring the customer to tender an amount greater than the cost. The shopkeeper would then have to work out the correct change.

Ma 2/3bc
MD/B1 AS/B1 M/B1 PSE

Textbook Pages 17 and 18 *Using the 2 and 3 times tables including money*

Page 17 provides word problems. In Question 2 some children may need to be guided to look at the illustrations for the essential information.

Page 18 provides money examples. If the introductory activities have been carried out the children should have little difficulty with Questions 1 and 2. If appropriate they should be warned of any prices which differ from the prices used for the same items on sale in the class shop. Coins should be available for use if required.

In Question 1 parts (g) to (i) the children might find it helpful to record the costs of the different articles separately before adding to find a total cost.

$$\begin{array}{r} 18p \\ \underline{9p} \\ 27p \end{array}$$

Problem solving

Questions 3 and 4 are more demanding and involve problem solving. Questions 3 and 4 (b) are essentially of the type '3 times what equals 15p?', and might be verbalised in this way by some children.

THE 4 TIMES TABLE
Introductory activities

Ma 2/3bc 1/3a 3/3a
AS/B1 MD/B1 M/B1

The 2 and 3 times tables were built up using concrete materials. While the 4 times table could also be built up in this way, more emphasis should be placed on finding the answer by repeated addition, for example,

4×8, 4 times 8, or 4 eights $= 8 + 8 + 8 + 8 = 32$

The School context is continued by relating the work to a Lunchtime scenario.

1 Building up the table

Cherries in slices of cake

Use card cut-outs and counters.

'Put 1 cherry in each cake.
We have 4 ones.'

Write $4 \times 1 = 1 + 1 + 1 + 1 = 4$

'Put another cherry in each cake.
We have 4 twos.'

Write $4 \times 2 = 2 + 2 + 2 + 2 = 8$

Repeat for 4×3, 4×4, and 4×5.

By the time 4×6 is reached it is hoped that most children will be able to find the answer without having to put out cherries but by writing

$4 \times 6 = 6 + 6 + 6 + 6 = 24$

Point out that the answers to the 4 times table are increasing by 4 each time.

$4 \times 5 = 20$ so $4 \times 6 = 20 + 4 = 24$

Remember to include the zero fact.

$4 \times 0 = 0 + 0 + 0 + 0 = 0$

The previous activity could be repeated using

■ 'currants' in buns or drawings of currants in buns

    $4 \times 2 = 2 + 2 + 2 + 2 = 8$

■ interlocking cubes $4 \times 2 = 2 + 2 + 2 + 2 = 8$

2 Using the table

■ Work similar to that outlined on Page 93 for the 2 times table should be done with the 4 times table.

■ Use the class shop with items priced up to 10p. Ask the children to find the cost of 4 of any one item. Double purchases and giving change could be included as before.

Workbook 2 Pages 11 and 12   *The 4 times table*

On Page 11 make sure that the children realise that for 4×6 they are expected to write $4 \times 6 = 6 + 6 + 6 + 6 = 24$. They are not expected to draw pictures for all the facts.

Once all the facts have been found the children could be shown how to check using a calculator. For example,

Press [4] [×] [6] [=] to check that the answer is 24.

This may be the first time that the [×] key has been used.

On Page 12, Question 4 may be difficult for some children.

$4 \times \Box = 20$ should be read as '4 whats are 20'? The children's ability to answer depends on how well they know the 4 times table.

THE 5 TIMES TABLE
Introductory activities

The activities suggested for the 4 times table could be extended for the 5 times table. The School context is continued by relating the work to a Garden scenario.

1 Building up the table
This could be done by:

Putting seeds in trays
Use counters. Put 2 seeds in each tray.

$5 \times 2 = 2 + 2 + 2 + 2 + 2 = 10$

Drawing bulbs in bags
$5 \times 3 = 3 + 3 + 3 + 3 + 3 = 15$

Examples such as 5×7 could either be found by repeated addition without using material, for example,

$5 \times 7 = 7 + 7 + 7 + 7 + 7 = 35$

or by realising that 5 is added to the previous answer:

$5 \times 6 = 30$ so $5 \times 7 = 30 + 5 = 35$

2   Using the table

■ Work similar to that outlined on Page 93, for the 2 times table should be done with the 5 times table.

■ Sequences of the 5 times table are rather special. Oral activities could be related to children's games where counting in fives is often used to start a game.

> 5, 10, 15, 20, __, __, __, __.
> 35, 30, 25, __, __, __, __, 0.
> 35, 40, 45, __, __, __, __, __.

The children should be encouraged to continue this sequence beyond 50.

Ma 2/3b 3/3a
MD/B1 AS/B1 PS/B2

Workbook 2 Pages 13 and 14   *The 5 times table*

On Page 13 the children have to check answers using a calculator.

On Page 14, Question 4, some children might have to be shown the starting number in each sequence.

USING THE 4 AND 5 TIMES TABLES INCLUDING MONEY
Introductory activities

Ma 2/3bc 1/3a
MD/B1 AS/B1 M/B1

Class shop

A section of the class shop could be set up to display articles associated with a Garden Centre, for example, bulbs, labels, plants and flowers. These should be labelled with prices up to 10p. Ask the children to find the cost of 5 of any one item. Double purchases and giving change could be included as before.

Ma 2/3abc
MD/B1 AS/B1

Workbook 2 Pages 15 and 16   *Using the 4 and 5 times tables*

The children have to interpret information from pictures and use the appropriate table to find the answers.

Page 15, Question 2 might cause some difficulty.

Page 16 contains money work which is extended in Question 2 to giving change.

John had	50p
He bought 4 daisies	20p
His change was	30p

The change is expected to be found by subtraction. Some children might find the change mentally by 'adding on'.

THE 2, 3, 4 AND 5 TIMES TABLES
Additional activities

A range of activities could be used to allow the children to practise the tables facts.

1 Clock game
Prepare a modified clock face as shown, inserting the table number in the middle of the face. Point, for example, to 8.
The child should respond

'2 times 8 is 16.'

or

'2 eights are 16.'

The response might be shortened to give the product '16' only.

2 Triples game   *(for 2 to 4 players)*
Prepare a playing board, as shown, and 3 sets of numeral cards numbered from 1 to 10. Shuffle the cards and place face down. Give each player a set of coloured counters, each player having a different colour.

3	6	9	12	15
30	27	24	21	18
18	21	24	27	30
15	12	9	6	3

Each player in turn takes a card from the shuffled pack. A player finds 3 times the number on the card and covers the product on the board with a counter. The answer could be checked using a calculator. The game is finished when all the numbers on the board are covered or after a time limit has elapsed. The winner is the player who has covered most numbers.

3 Bees and flowers
Ask some children to make flowers and others to make bees. Tables facts could be written on the flowers and numbers on the bees. The children display these with each bee on or beside its correct flower.

4 Crocodiles
Make a '5 times' crocodile using the numbers 1 to 10, as shown.

A child has to walk along the crocodile's back to cross a river. To progress he/she must correctly multiply each number by 5. Each child in turn attempts the walk. When a mistake is made the child stays at that number and awaits another turn. Answers could be checked using a calculator.

5 Multiplication grids

Grids like this could be made for any table for the children to complete.

5 times	4	8	3	9	0	6	10	1	5	2	7
	20										

6 Number cards

Prepare yellow cards such as | 2 × 3 | | 3 × 5 | | 4 × 6 | | 5 × 8 |

Prepare matching blue cards such as | 6 | | 15 | | 24 | | 40 |

These cards could be used in several ways:

- The yellow cards could be displayed to give written or oral practice as appropriate.

- Yellow and blue cards could be mixed face down on a desk top. Each player in turn picks one card of each colour. If the cards match, for example, | 4 × 7 | and | 28 |, the player keeps the pair of cards and continues picking cards.

If the cards do not match, the player replaces them face down. Two or more children could play this game. The winner is the child who collects most matching pairs.

THE COMMUTATIVE LAW FOR MULTIPLICATION
Introductory activities

Ma 2/3bc
MD/B1

The commutative law for addition was introduced in Heinemann Mathematics 1. It is important that children are aware that this law applies to multiplication as well as to addition, for example,

$$4 \times 3 = 3 \times 4$$

Although the physical representations of 4×3 and 3×4 may look different the products are the same. Knowledge of this property is most useful for finding facts in the later tables and so reduces the number of multiplication facts which children have to memorise.

1 Using interlocking cubes

Put out 4 threes 4×3

Put out 3 fours 3×4

From the cubes it can be seen that $4 \times 3 = 3 \times 4$.

The children should be asked to do other examples. Initially these should be restricted within 5×5 so that both forms are within known tables. Once the children have mastered this they could progress to using cubes for an example like 3×8 and 8×3 where 8×3 is an unknown table fact from the 8 times table, which is dealt with in Heinemann Mathematics 4.

2 Using counters and straws

An array of 12 counters could be
separated in 2 ways as shown.
Emphasise that $3 \times 4 = 4 \times 3$.

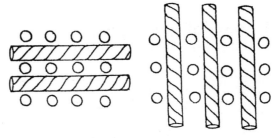

3 Using pegs and a pegboard

A similar arrangement to that shown for counters and straws could be shown with
pegs on a pegboard.

4 Using number lines

Children could use pairs of prepared number lines to show the jumps.

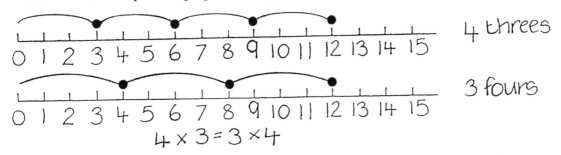

4 threes

3 fours

$4 \times 3 = 3 \times 4$

Workbook 2 Pages 17 and 18 *Commutative aspect*

Ma 2/3b
MD/B1

The School context is continued by relating the work to the Library.

It is essential that some prior teaching and discussion take place as outlined
above, before children try Page 17. Make sure they know what to write in
Question 1, i.e. $2 \times 4 = 4 \times 2$ and $5 \times 3 = 3 \times 5$, and that in Question 2 they use
the number lines correctly.

Page 18, Question 1 involves drawing spots on 2 sets of 'worms'. Ensure that
the children see the relationship between the pairs of drawings each time.

Question 2 uses the commutative law to explore facts in tables beyond the
5 times table. Two distractors, 5×4 and 2×9, are included in the set.

THE 10 TIMES TABLE AND ONE HUNDRED
Introductory activities

Ma 2/2a 2/3b 1/3b 3/3a
MD/B1 RTN/B1

The 2, 3, 4, and 5 times tables were built up using repeated addition. The 10 times
table could be built up in a similar fashion but the work becomes somewhat tedious,
for example,

$10 \times 7 = 7 + 7 + 7 + 7 + 7 + 7 + 7 + 7 + 7 + 7 = 70$

A different approach using the commutative law for multiplication and a knowledge
of place value is suggested.

1 Introducing the 10 times table

The idea is that 10×6, (10 sixes) is found by writing 10×6 as 6×10.
6×10 is then read as 6 tens.
6 tehs from place value knowledge is known to be 60.

So $10 \times 6 = 6 \times 10 = 6$ tens $= 60$.

This is the approach used on Workbook 2, Page 19, but it is strongly recommended that you and the children build up and discuss the table together, recording each step.

The pattern of answers 10, 20, 30, . . ., 90 should be highlighted.

A calculator could also be used to find the pattern.

Enter $\boxed{10}$ Press $\boxed{\times}$ $\boxed{3}$ $\boxed{=}$ to give 30 and so on.

2 Introducing one hundred

Care should be taken when introducing $10 \times 10 = 10$ tens. It will have to be explained that another way of expressing 10 tens is 1 hundred and that 1 hundred is written as 100. This is new work for these children.

The number 100 could also be seen on a calculator as follows:

Enter $\boxed{99}$ Press $\boxed{+}$ $\boxed{1}$ $\boxed{=}$ to give 100

The next number after 99 is 100.

Enter $\boxed{10}$ Press $\boxed{\times}$ $\boxed{1}$ $\boxed{0}$ $\boxed{=}$ to give 100

Further work on numbers greater than 100 is provided in Heinemann Mathematics 4.

Ma 2/3bc
MD/B1

Workbook 2 Page 19   *Building up the 10 times table*

The introductory activities outlined above should take place before the children try Page 19. Some children might still require help with the questions.

THE £1 COIN
Introductory activities

Ma 2/2ab
M/B1 AS/B1

The 50p coin and calculations involving addition and subtraction of money to 99p were introduced in Workbook 1. Now that the 10 times table has been built up, the opportunity is taken to introduce the £1 coin which is equivalent to ten 10p coins or 100p. This will thus extend the children's knowledge of the coins in daily use.

1 The £1 coin

Show the children a £1 coin and ask them to note any differences it has from other coins. The differences are in colour, thickness and edge and these should be highlighted for the children. The phrase 'ONE POUND' also appears on the 'tail' side.

The children could use real coins to make coin rubbings to show the designs on the head and tail sides.

The symbol '£' standing for 'pound' should be highlighted and its position before the number emphasised, as in '£3' standing for 'three pounds'. The children may well have seen this on display tickets in shops etc., but some practice in saying what various prices mean could be helpful, for example,

'How much is this?'   'Seven pounds.'

2 Counting out coins

Plastic, cardboard or real coins could be used for this work with the children.

■ Ask a group of children to use 10p coins to count in tens until they reach 100. Establish with them the fact that ten 10p coins = 100p. Explain how 100p has the same value as £1, hence the relationship,

   has the same value as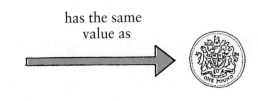

■ Ask the children to carry out different exchanging activities with these ten 10p coins. For example,

'Exchange two 10p coins for a 20p coin'.

    has the same value as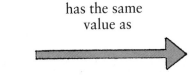

Ask the children to check by counting '20, 40, ... 100'.

'Exchange five 10p coins for a 50p coin.'

    has the same value as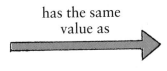

Ask the children to check by counting '50 and 50 is 100'.

■ Each time an exchange is made the £1 equivalent should be highlighted. Ask questions:

'How many 10p or 20p or 50p coins have the same value as £1?'

■ Ask the children to use different sets of coins to make up £1. For example,

Ask the children to check by counting '50, 70, 90,100'.

Highlight the £1 equivalence each time.

3 Using £1 coins

Use price tickets for items and ask the children to put out £1 coins to pay for the items. Prices like these are used in Workbook 2, Page 22, Question 1.

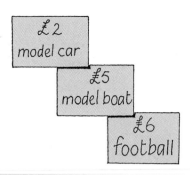

£2 model car
£5 model boat
£6 football

Ma 2/2ba
M/B1 AS/B1

> ## Workbook 2 Page 20 *Introducing the £1 coin*
>
> The work on Page 20 uses the scenario of a Book Sale and buying a bundle of books for £1. It provides a check up on the introductory activities suggested above.
>
> In Question 3 the children need not draw life-size coins for their answers. It would be sufficient to show a coin value as (50p) or (20p) .

USING THE 2, 3, 4, 5 AND 10 TIMES TABLES INCLUDING MONEY
Introductory activities

Ma 2/3bc
MD/B1 AS/B1 PS/B2

1 Activities and games

Some of the activities and games listed in the additional activities for the 2, 3, 4, and 5 times tables on Page 99 would be worthwhile introductory activities to the pages which follow.

2 Oral work

A short period of oral work with a group of children should precede any written work.

Workbook 2, Pages 21–24 and Textbook Pages 19 and 20 are set in the context of 'going home from school'. Activities and games in which the children might be involved outside school or at home are included.

Ma 2/3bc 1/3bc 3/2a
MD/B1 AS/B2 PS/B1

Extension

> ## Workbook 2 Pages 21 and 22 *2, 3, 4, 5 and 10 times tables*
>
> The context of catching a bus should be discussed with the children. On Page 22, Question 1, some children may need to write down the cost of 5 skirts and then the cost of 5 shirts in order to find the total cost.
>
> Page 22, Question 2 requires a considerable amount of calculation.
>
> In Question 4 some children may need to be reminded about odd and even numbers. The additions to, and subtractions from, the multiplication facts are expected to be done mentally. This work is required for the game on Workbook 2, Pages 23 and 24.

Workbook 2 Pages 23 and 24   *2, 3, 4, 5 and 10 times tables*

This game for 2–4 players provides practice in using the 2, 3, 4, 5 and 10 times tables. It is based on walking home from school by road. A dice, counters, calculator and coloured pencil or crayon are needed. One child's workbook pages are used for any one game.

How to play

1 Each player chooses a number trail (shown at the side of each page) and a counter.

2 Each player in turn throws the dice, moves forward the appropriate number of boxes and gives an answer to the calculation stated in the box on which the counter lands.

3 The answer is checked on the calculator by another player, or a referee (a child not actually playing the game).

■ If the answer is correct, then all players with that number on their number trail colour the number.

■ If the answer is wrong the player goes back 2 places and awaits another turn.

Pedestrian crossings
These are used only for going 'up' the board. If a counter lands at the 'bottom' of a crossing then the player must answer the calculation correctly before moving up the crossing.

Speed limit signs

For a sign like ⓣ⓪ a player must state 2 numbers which when multiplied

together give 40, for example, 10×4, 4×10, or 5×8.

■ If the answer is correct, then that sign number should be coloured on the appropriate number trails.

■ If the answer is wrong the player goes back 2 places and awaits another turn.

Boxes with + and – signs

■ If a counter lands on a '+' box the player is given an extra turn.

■ If a counter lands on a '–' box the player misses a turn.

Finding the winner

One of the following ways should be selected:

■ The first player to reach home.

■ The player with most numbers coloured on his/her number trail after playing for a set time.

■ The player with most numbers coloured on his/her number trail after *all* players have reached home. (This may take some considerable time.)

Note that a draw is possible in the last two ways.

Textbook Pages 19 and 20   *2, 3, 4, 5 and 10 times tables*

The context of the At home activities on Pages 19 and 20 should be discussed with the children.

On Page 19, Question 3, the children will probably need to set out vertical additions in order to find answers.

In the darts exemplar on Page 20 it should be pointed out to the children that two darts in section 7 means (2×7).

In Question 2 it should be emphasised that 3 darts have to be used each time. There is more than one answer for some numbers. For example,

$$22 = (2 \times 8) + 6 \quad \text{or} \quad 22 = (2 \times 7) + 8$$

The exemplar given for Question 3 should be discussed with the children so that they realise that:

■ not all the keys indicated need be used each time

For example,   15 = 3 × 5

■ some keys may be used more than once

For example,   4 = 2 × 2

27 = 3 × 3 × 3

■ more than three keys could be used

For example   60 = 2 × 5 × 2 × 3

The answers are found essentially by trial and error. The children should be encouraged to record their trials each time.

Textbook Page 21   *Other activity: positioning*

■ This page could be attempted at any time.

■ The children could work individually or in pairs. Some preliminary work and discussion with the children about the phrases used in Question 2 may be necessary. For example, arrange 4 children sitting at a table. Ask, for example,

'Who is opposite Ann?'

'Who is on Carol's right?'

'Who is between Ann and Carol?'

When you are satisfied with the children's responses, they could be asked to attempt the work on Page 21.

Name cards could be made to help the children with Question 2.

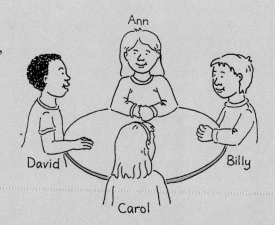

Additional activity

Ask 6 children to sit at a table so that

  Emma is opposite Hari

  Ian is on Hari's left

  Jason in between Ian and Emma

  Gerald is opposite Jason

  Farida is next to Gerald

Other appropriate phrases could be used.

Division: Sharing

Overview

This section

- introduces the concept of division by sharing, including remainders
- introduces the use of the ÷ symbol for sharing examples
- introduces the link between division and multiplication

	Teacher's Notes	Workbook 2	Textbook
Concept of division : equal sharing	110	25, 26	
Division: sharing using the ÷ symbol	111	27, 28	
Division: sharing with remainders	112	29	22
Linking division and multiplication	113	30	

Key words and phrases

Share equally between   How many in each?   remainder
Share equally among   How many left over?

Resources

Useful materials

- cubes or counters
- dice
- 'remainder box' for sharing game
- other materials suggested within the introductory activities
- flashcards of key words and phrases

Assessment and Resources Pack

Assessment

Check-ups

Check-up 4
Workbook 2 Pages 25–30
(Division: sharing)

Resources

Resource Cards

Resource Cards 22 to *24* (Clothes
show) can be used for sharing
activities.

Teaching notes

The context: on holiday

All the work in the division sections and the fraction section is based on a Holiday theme. Adults and children prepare to go on holiday and journey to a seaside resort where they visit the beach and the harbour. Some preliminary discussion should take place about going on holiday and holiday activities.

CONCEPT OF DIVISION

There are two aspects to division, namely equal sharing and grouping. The following examples illustrate these two aspects.

Equal sharing

Share 8 apples equally between 2 boys. How many does each receive?

The answer is found by sharing the apples, giving one to each alternately until none are left, and then counting *how many are in each share*.

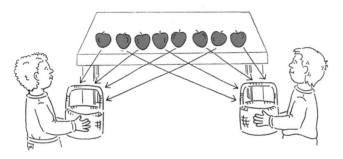

The answer is *4 apples*.

Grouping

From a bag of 8 apples, how many girls can each receive 2 apples?

Here the answer is found by grouping the apples in twos, repeatedly subtracting from 8, and then counting *the number of girls* to whom apples have been given.

The answer is *4 girls*.

CONCEPT OF DIVISION: EQUAL SHARING
Introductory activities

Ma 2/3c 1/3b
MD/B1

To introduce the sharing aspect of division, the children should be asked to share material such as cubes or counters and then count the number in each share to find the answer.

Initially sharing should be done 'between' 2 and later 'among' 3, 4 and 5. The examples should have no remainders and the answers given orally.

1 Children and cars

Put out two sets of four chairs to represent seats in a car.

'Share 6 children equally between the 2 cars. How many children are in each car?'

Ask 6 children to sit alternately in the two cars.

Ask   'How many children?'(6)
       'How many cars?'(2)
       'How many in each car?'(3)

'6 children shared equally between 2 cars gives 3 children to each car.'

Repeat this activity with 4 children.

2 Eggs in pans

The children could make eggs from paper or card. Paper plates could be used for pans.

'Share 8 eggs equally among 4 pans. How many eggs in each pan?'

Ask the children to share 8 eggs among 4 pans.

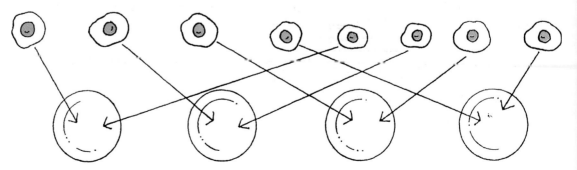

Ask   'How many eggs?'(8)
       'How many pans?'(4)
       'How many eggs in each pan?'(2)

  '8 eggs shared equally among 4 pans gives 2 eggs in each pan.'

Repeat this activity for other numbers of eggs and pans.

3   Other activities

Activities similar to those above could be done using

■ pennies in purses

■ shells in tubs

■ fish in pools

Workbook **2**

Ma 2/3c 1/3b
MD/B1

Workbook 2 Pages 25 and 26   *Division: equal sharing*

Pages 25 and 26 use the Holiday theme and relate to the journey to, and arrival at, a campsite. The answers should be found practically using cubes or counters. For example on Page 25, Question 1, 10 counters, representing the T-shirts should be shared between, and placed on, the 2 cases, so that it can be seen that there are 5 T-shirts for each case.

DIVISION: SHARING USING THE ÷ SYMBOL
Introductory activities

Similar activities to those suggested for introducing the concept of division by sharing should be carried out to introduce the division symbol.

Ma 1/3b 2/3c
MD/B1

1   Introducing the ÷ symbol

Having carried out a practical sharing activity, for example, '8 cakes shared equally among 4 plates gives 2 cakes on each plate', explain how this can be written using symbols, i.e. $8 \div 4 = 2$ where '÷' means *shared equally among*.

Give the children examples which have to be recorded using the '÷' symbol.

2   Pick a card

Prepare a set of division cards such as $\boxed{18 \div 3}$ $\boxed{10 \div 2}$ etc

Ask a child to pick a card, verbalise the question using sharing language, and find the answer practically.

Having found the answer to, for example $\boxed{10 \div 2}$, the child would say '10 shared

equally between 2 is 5' and write $10 \div 2 = 5$.

Repeat for other cards.

DIVISION: SHARING WITH REMAINDERS
Introductory activities

1 Shells in pails

Give the children practical problems such as 'Share 14 shells equally among 4 pails. How many shells are in each pail?'

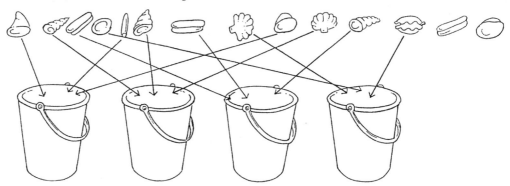

Place 1 shell in each pail in turn until there are not enough shells left to give another 1 to each pail.

Say '14 shells shared equally among 4 pails gives 3 to each pail and there are 2 shells left over'.

Explain to the children that the number of shells 'left over' is called the *remainder* and that we say:

'14 shared equally among 4 is 3 remainder 2' and write 14 ÷ 4 = 3 r 2.

Repeat for other examples.

2 Pick a card

Prepare a set of cards such as $\boxed{13 \div 3}$ $\boxed{11 \div 2}$ etc.

Ask a child to pick a card, verbalise the question using sharing language and find the answer practically.

Having found the answer to, for example $\boxed{13 \div 3}$, the child would say '13 shared equally among 3 is 4 remainder 1' and write $13 \div 3 = 4$ r 1.

Repeat for other cards.

Workbook **2**

Ma 2/3c 1/3b
MD/B1

Workbook 2 Page 29   *Division: sharing with remainders*

The children should verbalise each example using sharing language and find each answer practically. Not all examples involve remainders.

In Question 3 the children have to write 'r' for remainder in some examples.

LINKING DIVISION AND MULTIPLICATION
Introductory activities

Ma 2/3c 3/3b
MD/B1

The link between division and multiplication should be shown to the children practically using cubes and trays.

'Share 12 cubes equally among 3 trays to give 4 cubes in each tray.'

$\boxed{12 \div 3 = 4}$

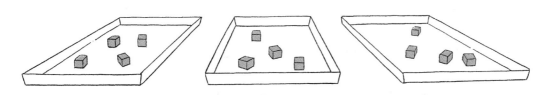

The drawing also shows 3 lots of 4 cubes giving 12 cubes.

$\boxed{12 \div 3 = 4}$

Repeat for other examples using cubes and trays.

Ma 2/3c 3/3b
MD/B1

Workbook 2 Page 30   *Linking division and multiplication*

In Questions 1–4, each drawing shows the result of a sharing activity, which has to be recorded. Each drawing has then to be interpreted as a multiplication and the answer recorded.

Textbook Page 22 *Division game: sharing*

This track game for 4 children provides practice in making equal shares. Sometimes there will be a remainder.

Each player needs 10 cubes, a counter and a track (Page 22). However, a track could be shared. The group will also need a dice and a box known as the 'remainder box'.

The aim of the game is for a player to get rid of all of his or her cubes.

How to play

1 Each player rolls the dice and moves his or her counter the relevant number of spaces.

2 If the space on which the dice lands shows a number

- the player makes that number of equal shares from his or her cubes. For example, if the space shows 3, then the player makes 3 equal shares.

- any cubes left over are placed in the remainder box.

- the player keeps one share and distributes the other shares, one to each of the other players of his/her choice. The children will gradually realise that shares should be given to those players with fewest cubes.

3 If the space on which the dice lands gives instructions about putting cubes in the remainder box, the player does this.

4 ■ If a player has fewer cubes than allows shares to be formed, for example, a player has 3 cubes to be shared among 4 then the 3 cubes are placed in the remainder box and that player is the winner.

- If a player is asked, for example, to place 3 cubes in the remainder box and only has 2, these are placed in the box and that player is the winner.

Fractions: Halves and quarters

Ma 1/3b
Ma 2/2c
RTN/A2,B2
FPR/B1

Overview

This section

- introduces the notation for halves and quarters
- gives methods of finding 'one half of' and 'one quarter of' a set of objects

	Teacher's Notes	Workbook 2	Textbook
Fractions: notation $\frac{1}{2}$ and $\frac{1}{4}$	116	31	
Fractions : notation $\frac{2}{2}$, $\frac{2}{4}$, $\frac{3}{4}$, $\frac{4}{4}$	117	32	
'One half of' and 'one quarter of' a set	118	33, 34	

Key words and phrases

equal parts	halves	quarters	two quarters
fraction	halved	quartered	three quarters
one half of	one half	one quarter	four quarters
	two halves	one quarter of	

Resources

Useful materials

- coloured pencils
- interlocking cubes
- other materials suggested within the introductory activities
- flashcards of key words and fractions

Assessment and Resources Pack

Assessment

Check-ups

Check-up 5
Workbook 2 Pages 31–34
(Halves and quarters)

Assessment in Context

Assessment in Context 3
The dream

Resources

Problem Solving Activities
11 Postcard puzzle (Fractions)

Teaching notes

FRACTIONS: NOTATION $\frac{1}{2}$ AND $\frac{1}{4}$
Introductory activities

Ma 2/2c 1/3b
RTN/A2,B2

The concepts of one half and one quarter were introduced in Heinemann Mathematics 2. The notation for one half and one quarter is now introduced.

1 The notation for 'one half'

Ask the children to fold a paper rectangle in half. Discuss two ways of doing this. Write 'one half' on each part, as shown.

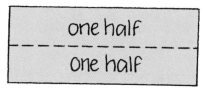
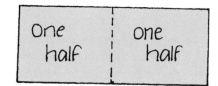

Emphasise that, for halves, a shape must be divided into 2 equal parts, each of the 2 equal parts is known as 'one half' and two halves make the whole.

Introduce the notation $\frac{1}{2}$ for a half explaining that a half is 1 part out of 2 equal parts and is written $\frac{1}{2}$.

Ask the children to fold shapes into two equal parts and write $\frac{1}{2}$ on each part.

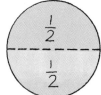

2 The notation for 'one quarter'

Ask the children to fold a paper rectangle into quarters and write 'one quarter' on each part, as shown.

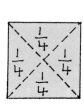

Emphasise that, for quarters, a shape must be divided into 4 equal parts, each of the 4 equal parts is called 'one quarter' and four quarters make the whole.

Guide the children towards finding a notation for one quarter,. i.e. one quarter is 1 part out of 4 equal parts and is written $\frac{1}{4}$. Ask them to fold other shapes into quarters and write $\frac{1}{4}$ on each part.

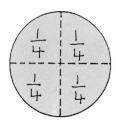

A Picnic at the beach continues the Holiday theme.

In Questions 2 and 4 remind the children that the sandwiches ticked have to have 2 and 4 *equal* parts respectively.

Question 5 may need to be discussed with the children.

FRACTIONS : NOTATION $\frac{2}{2}$, $\frac{2}{4}$, $\frac{3}{4}$, $\frac{4}{4}$
Introductory activities

1   Folding activities

■ Ask the children to fold and annotate a rectangle, as shown

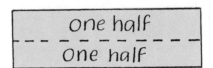

Emphasise that two halves make one whole, and show that '2 halves' is written as $\frac{2}{2}$.

■ Ask the children to fold a circle into quarters and
colour two quarters. Show that 2 quarters is written as $\frac{2}{4}$.

Guide the children towards finding a notation for 3 quarters and 4 quarters.

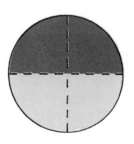

Ma 2/2c 1/3b
RTN/A2,B2

2   Cards

Make two sets of cards, one set using drawings of fractions of shapes like this:

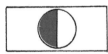

the other set using words like these:

one half	two halves	one quarter	two quarters	three quarters	four quarters

Provide a set of blank cards and ask the children to write the corresponding notation on each. This gives a pack of 18 cards altogether. The children could then match each notation card to its equivalents in the other two sets.

3   Snap

Two packs of the cards made in Activity 2 could be used to play a game of Snap. A snap situation occurs when two cards played in sequence show one of the following:

■ an illustration and the matching words

■ an illustration and the matching notation

■ words and the matching notation

Ma 2/2c 1/3b
RTN/A2,B2

The answers to Question 4 should be written in fraction notation.

'ONE HALF OF' AND 'ONE QUARTER OF' A SET
Introductory activities

Ma 2/2c 1/2b 1/3b
RTN/A2,B2 FPR/B1

Finding 'one half of' or 'one quarter of' a set could be done

■ visually

■ by reference to the previous work dealing with halving or quartering one whole

■ by sharing

1   Visual perception

Sometimes 'one half of' and 'one quarter of' a set of objects can be found visually. For example, by looking at the carton of 6 eggs shown it can be seen that $\frac{1}{2}$ of 6 = 3 because the two parts of the box are the same, each containing three eggs.

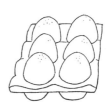

Show the children sets of objects arranged symmetrically and ask them to find 'one half of' and 'one quarter of' visually.

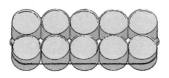

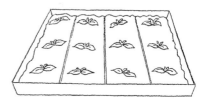

10 cans altogether in the pack
(5 cans in each half of pack)
$\frac{1}{2}$ of 10 = 5.

12 plants altogether in the tray
(3 plants in each quarter of tray)
$\frac{1}{4}$ of 12 = 3.

2   Linking with a fraction of one whole

Using whole shapes or objects which have been marked off into an even number of equal parts, the following practical activities could be carried out with the children to find 'one half of'.

Squared paper

Use 2 cm squared paper. Ask a child to count the total number of squares, for example 8, fold the piece of paper so that it is halved, and count the number of squares in one half, 4.

One half of 8 is 4.

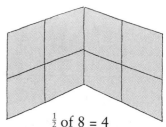

$\frac{1}{2}$ of 8 = 4

Interlocking cubes

Ask a child to link together 10 interlocking cubes to make a tower, break this into 2 equal parts, match the lengths to check that the two parts are equal, and count the number in one part, 5.

One half of 10 is 5.

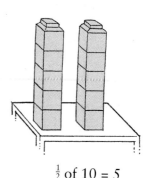

$\frac{1}{2}$ of 10 = 5

Bars of chocolate or biscuits

A similar activity could be done using a bar of chocolate or a biscuit as shown.

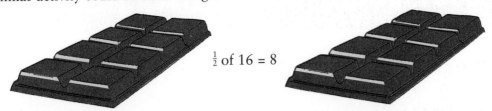

$\frac{1}{2}$ of 16 = 8

Finding 'one quarter of' can be done in a similar way, ensuring that the whole is made up of a number of equal parts which is a multiple of four.

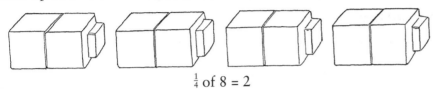

$\frac{1}{4}$ of 8 = 2

3 Sharing

This method is explored more fully in Heinemann Mathematics 4 which deals with the relationship between 'a fraction of' and 'shared equally among'. For example, $\frac{1}{2}$ of 10 is equivalent to $10 \div 2$.

At this stage some practical work might be undertaken to establish that, for example, sharing a number of objects between two is linked with finding one half of a number of objects.

For example, share 10 cubes between 2 by laying them out in 2 rows, *one to each in turn.*

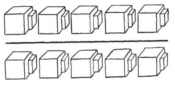

The set of cubes is then seen to be halved showing that $\frac{1}{2}$ of 10 = 5.

Workbook 2 Pages 33 and 34   *Half and quarter of a set*

Th Beach Shop continues the Holiday theme.

Page 33 deals with finding 'one half of' a set.

In Question1, the approach is visual where the child 'sees' one half of the whole and counts the number in one half.

In Question 2, the child should make a row or tower of cubes, break this into 2 equal parts and count the number of cubes in one part.

Cubes should be used to represent the stamps in Question 3 and the postcards in Question 4. The answers are found as in Question 2.

Page 34 deals with finding 'one quarter of' a set and is similar to Page 33.

Ma 1/3abcd
Ma 2/3c
Ma 3/2a
MD/B1
AS/B1
PS/B1
PSE

Division: Grouping

Overview

This section

■ introduces the concept of division by grouping, including remainders

■ introduces the use of the ÷ symbol for grouping examples

	Teacher's Notes	Workbook 2	Textbook
Concept of division: grouping	120	35, 36	
Division: grouping using the ÷ symbol	122	37	
Division: grouping with remainders	123	38	
Other activities			23–26
Extension		38	26
Problem solving			25, 26

Key words and phrases

How many groups?   Make groups of
Ring groups of   remainder

Resources

Useful materials

■ cubes or counters

■ other materials suggested within the introductory activities

■ flashcards of key words and phrases

Assessment and Resources Pack

Assessment

Check-ups

Check-up 6
Workbook 2 Pages 35–38
(Division : grouping)

Check-up 7
Workbook 2 Pages 1–38
(×, ÷; halves, quarters)

Assessment in Context

Assessment Context 4
Max

Assessment Context 5
Cascades shopping centre

Resources

Resource Cards

Resource Cards 21 to 23 (Clothes show) can be used for grouping activities.

Teaching Notes

CONCEPT OF DIVISION: GROUPING
Introductory activities

This second section of work on division deals with grouping. The children should be given practical experience of grouping objects involving the Holiday theme if possible. The examples should have no remainders and the answers should be given orally.

Ma 2/3c 1/3b
MD/B

1   Beach games
'How many groups of 3 can be made from 12 children?'

Choose 12 children and ask them to group themselves in threes.

Ask   'How many children?'*(12)*
      'How many in each group?'*(3)*
      'How many groups?' *(4)*

   '12 children grouped in threes gives 4 groups.'

Repeat this activity, making groups of 4 and 6.

2   A picnic
'There are 20 sandwiches. How many children can be given 4 each?'

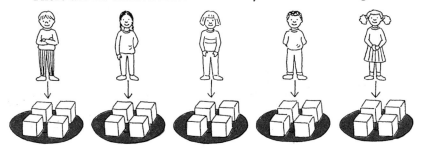 

Use cubes to represent sandwiches and give 4 to each child in turn until all 20 cubes are given out.

Ask   'How many sandwiches?'*(20)*
      'How many to each child?'*(4)*
      'How many children get sandwiches?'*(5)*

   '20 sandwiches grouped in fours gives 5 groups.'

Repeat this for different numbers of sandwiches.

121

3 Number line

Use the classroom number line to count equal groups.

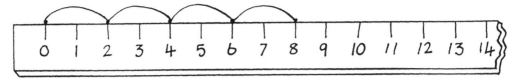

'How many twos are there in 8?'

'Start from 0. Make jumps of 2 until you reach 8, counting each jump as you go.'

'8 grouped in twos gives 4 groups.'

Alternatively children could start from 8 and count back in twos.

4 Rings

Give children drawings of items related to the Holiday theme and ask them to ring groups of 2, 3, 4 and so on.

'Ring groups of 5 deckchairs.'

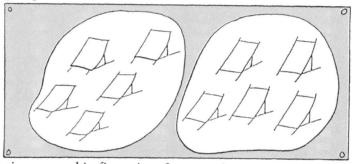

'10 chairs grouped in fives gives 2 groups.'

Ma 2/3c
MD/B1

Workbook 2 Pages 35 and 36   *Division: concept of grouping*

These pages continue the Holiday theme and are related to Beach activities. The answers should be found practically using counters or cubes.

For example on Page 35, Question 2, 2 counters are placed on each swing until all the counters are used up. The number of swings having 2 counters is the number of groups of two.

The drawings of swings, boats and chairs could be used, with counters, for other grouping examples not given on the pages.

DIVISION: GROUPING USING THE ÷ SYMBOL
Introductory activities

Ma 1/3b 2/3c
MD/B1

Activities similar to those suggested for introducing the concept of division by grouping should be carried out to introduce the ÷ symbol.

1 Introducing the ÷ symbol

Having carried out a practical grouping activity, for example, '15 chairs grouped in threes gives 5 groups', explain how this can be written using symbols, i.e. $15 \div 3 = 5$ where '÷' means 'grouped in'.

Give the children examples which have to be recorded using the '÷' symbol.

2 Pick a card

Prepare a set of division cards such as $\boxed{15 \div 5}$ $\boxed{12 \div 4}$ etc.

Ask a child to pick a card, verbalise the question using grouping language, and find the answer practically.

Having found the answer to, say $\boxed{12 \div 4}$ the child would say '12 grouped in fours gives 3 groups' and write $12 \div 4 = 3$.

Repeat for other cards.

Ma 2/3c
MD/B1

Workbook 2 Page 37 *Division: grouping using the ÷ symbol*

The Harbour scene should be discussed with the children.

The answers to Questions 1–4 are found by ringing groups of objects and counting the number of groups ringed.

For the examples in Question 5, the children should interpret for example, $24 \div 3$, as 24 grouped in threes.

DIVISION: GROUPING WITH REMAINDERS
Introductory activities

Give the children a few practical problems involving remainders.

Ma 2/3c 1/3b
MD/B1

1 Boats

Draw chalk outlines on the floor or use large paper cut-outs to represent boats. Ask 14 children to arrange themselves so that there are 4 in each boat. Discuss the result.

'Only 3 boats have 4 children in each. 2 children are left over.'

Remind the children that the number left over is called the *remainder*.

We say '14 grouped in fours is 3 remainder 2' and write $14 \div 4 = 3$ r 2.'

Repeat for other numbers of children.

2 Books

Ask the children to group books. For example:

'Put 17 books in groups of 5.'

'How many groups?' *(3)*
'How many left over ?'*(2)*

$17 \div 5 = 3 \text{ r } 2.$

3 Pick a card

Prepare a set of cards such as $\boxed{11 \div 3}$ $\boxed{13 \div 5}$ etc.

Ask a child to pick a card, verbalise the question using grouping language and find the answer practically.

Having found the answer to, for example $\boxed{7 \div 2}$, the child would say

'7 grouped in twos is 3 remainder 1 and write $7 \div 2 = 3 \text{ r } 1$.'

Repeat for other cards.

Ma 2/3c 1/3b
MD/B1

Extension

Workbook 2 Page 38 *Division: grouping with remainders*

In Question 2 the children have to write 'r' for remainder in some of the examples.

In Question 3, explain to the children that the boats have already been tied up in groups. To write the number story, the children have to count:

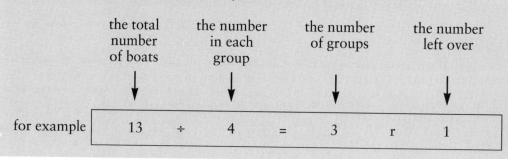

the total number of boats		the number in each group		the number of groups		the number left over
↓		↓		↓		↓
for example	13	÷	4	=	3	r	1

THE ÷ SYMBOL

The '÷' symbol has been used

- in the sharing aspect to mean 'shared equally among'
- in the grouping aspect to mean 'grouped in'

An example such as 15 ÷ 3 could be read as '15 divided by 3' and the answer found practically by using either a sharing or grouping method.

Textbook Page 23 *Other activity: repeated addition*

- This page could be attempted any time after the work on multiplication in Workbook 2. It complements the work done there on repeated addition.

- Some calculators have the following feature:

  If ⊞ ③ is entered, pressing ⊟ repeatedly will generate the sequence 3, 6, 9, 12, 15, 18, etc. The calculator has effectively been set up as an 'add 3 ' machine. Check whether the calculators used in your classroom have this feature.

- In Questions 1 and 2 this feature is introduced. In Questions 2 and 3 ensure that the children know how to check their answers.

Additional activity

The children could be encouraged to practise estimating and counting on by a task such as

'Enter ⑤ ⊞ ① into your calculator display. Now close your eyes and press ⊟ as often as you think you need to, to make the display show 11. Open your eyes and check to see if you have counted correctly.'

Textbook Page 24 *Other activity: repeated subtraction*

- This page could be attempted any time after the work in Workbook 2 on Division: concept of grouping, which is based on the idea of repeated subtraction.

- Some calculators have the following feature:

  If ① ⓪ ⊟ ② is entered, pressing the ⊟ repeatedly will generate the sequence 8, 6, 4, 2, 0. The calculator has effectively been set up as a 'subtract 2' machine. Check whether the calculators used in your classroom have this feature.

- In Question 1 and 2 this feature is introduced. In Questions 2 and 3 ensure that the children know how to check their answers.

Additional activity

The children could be encouraged to practise estimating and counting back by as task such as:

'Enter ⑦ ⊟ ① into your calculator display. Now close your eyes and press ⊟ as often as you think you need to, to make the display show 0. Open your eyes again and check to see whether you have counted correctly.'

Textbook page 25 *Other activity: adding odd and even numbers*

■ The work on Page 25, which involves the addition of odd and even numbers, may be attempted any time after the completion of the 'addition facts to 20' in Workbook 1.

■ The activity could be introduced by a brief discussion with the children to ensure they can identify and give examples of odd and even numbers.

■ It would be worthwhile to monitor the children's progress with Questions 2 and 3 to ensure they understand what is required and to check that the tables have been completed correctly before Question 4 is attempted. Some children will find the generalisations in Question 4 difficult.

Additional activity

The children's answers to Question 4 should be discussed, emphasising the use of the terms 'odd' and 'even' and the type of number obtained when odd and even, odd and odd , and even and even numbers are added. Some children may find it difficult to generalise.

Textbook Page 26 *Other activity: adding more than three numbers*

■ In this activity the children add more than three odd or even numbers to find the highest and lowest totals. Page 26 may be attempted any time after the 'addition of the tens and units' section in Workbook 1.

■ The children should be encouraged to study carefully the diagram at the top of the page and to note the 2 different paths. Some children might find it easier to obtain each total by pairing numbers which add to 10. For the path shown below, 2 could be added to 8.

In Question 1 it may have to be pointed out that in the last example there are 4 possible paths.

Questions 2 and 3 can be tackled by using a trial and error approach.

This workbook is divided into three separate mathematical sections. Further details for each section are given on the first page of the appropriate notes for that section.

	Teacher's Notes
Measure	pages 129–164
Shape	pages 165–187
Handling data	pages 188–197

- It is not intended that all the work in any one section be completed before other sections are started.
- Sections can be tackled in a different order to the order presented in the workbook.
- Teachers should ensure there is a good mix of measure, shape and handling data activities throughout each term.

Where possible, individual topics are contextualised but there is no overall theme for this workbook.

Measure, Shape and Handling data Workbook

MEASURE

This section contains six separate units dealing with various aspects of measure.
Details of the content, resources and language for each unit are given at the start of
the notes for that unit.

Ma 1/3ab
Ma 2/2d
Ma 2/3de
Ma 3/3a
Ma 5/3a
PSE
T/A3, B1,2,3,C3
PS/B2

Time

Overview

This section

■ revises reading hour and half-hour times on analogue and digital displays

■ introduces the concept of a minute

■ extends reading the time to include minutes past the hour on both digital and analogue displays

■ introduces the expressions 'quarter past' and 'quarter to' in terms of minutes past the hour

■ includes simple calculations of one hour before and one hour after as well as simple durations.

Key words and phrases

minute	hour	digital times	quarter past
one minute before	one hour before	timer	quarter to
one minute after	one hour after	time(s)	
minutes after	how many hours	same time	
minutes past			

Resources

Useful materials

- geared or real analogue clock
- digital clock or watch
- minute timer
- clockface stamp
- analogue and digital clocks made from card
- ball
- other materials suggested within the introductory activities
- flashcards of key words and phrases

Assessment and Resources Pack

Assessment

Check-ups

Check-up 1
MSHD Workbook Pages 1–7
(Time)

Resources

Problem Solving Activities
12 Time-up (Digital displays)

Resource Cards
Resource Cards 25 to 28 (Amazing)
involve analogue and digital times.

Teaching notes

REVISION OF HOURS AND HALF HOURS
Introductory activities

Ma 2/2d 2/3e 1/3b
T/A3,B2,3

O'clock and half past times were introduced in the Measure Workbook of
Heinemann Mathematics 2. Some further suggestions for practical work to revise
these are given below.

1 What time is it?

Ask the children to read (or write) the time shown on classroom clocks. Real clocks
or geared, plastic clocks or cardboard clocks could be used. A card 'mock-up' of the
front of a video recorder might be useful for displaying digital times.

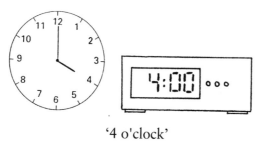

'4 o'clock'

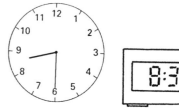

'half past 8'

2 Match the time

■ Give the children a time on an analogue
clock and ask them to find the matching
digital time from a set of prepared cards.

■ Give the children a digital time and ask
them to set the hands of an analogue
clock to give the same time.

3 Time game   *(for up to 4 players)*

The object of the game is for the children to collect pairs of
matching analogue and digital cards showing hours and half
hours.

Use a clockface stamp to make a set of
cards, each showing a given time.
Make a similar set of digital time cards
to match the analogue times. Mix the
two sets together.

Four cards are dealt to each child and the rest placed face down in a pile. In turn,
each child tries to collect a matching pair by choosing one card from the pile and
then discarding one card. A player may choose the discarded card of the previous
player instead of the unseen top card of the pile. The winner is the first child to
collect two pairs.

4 Postman's round

Make a set of cards to simulate mail collecting boxes. The children could put these in order of collection times.

Collect at	Collect at	Collect at	Collect at	Collect at
7:00	**7:30**	**8:00**	**8:30**	**9:00**
Baker Street	Cook Street	Fisher Street	Joiner Street	Painter Street

Ask questions such as

'Where did the postman go first (last) to collect the letters?'

'What time was the mail collected in Fisher Street?'

'At 9 o'clock, where would the postman be?' and so on.

Measure, Shape and Handling data Workbook **Page 1** *Time: revision of hours and half hours*

Ma 2/2d 2/3e
T/A3,B2,3

In Question 1, the children might require guidance in drawing the lines from the displays on the right and on the left to the words in the centre.

In Question 2, where the children have to write digital times, there is no need for them to imitate 'digital' numerals.

CONCEPT OF A MINUTE
Introductory activities

This section introduces the minute as a short interval of time and suggests activities which give the children experience of the duration of one minute.

Ma 2/3d 1/3b
T/B

1 Sitting silently for one minute

Indicate the start and finish of the time interval of one minute. Suggest to the children that they silently count 'one, two, three, . . .' over the period. This should help them with activities where the duration of a minute has to be estimated.

2 Estimating one minute

■ Ask the children to estimate when one minute of time has elapsed. At the start signal, the children could close their eyes and then put up their hands when they think one minute has passed. Counting silently to the appropriate number (see Activity 1) might help.

■ Signal the start and finish of time intervals which are significantly more or less than one minute. Ask

'Was that time more or less than a minute?'

3 What can you do in one minute?

The children could carry out a number of activities for a period of one minute:

- 'How many words can you copy?
- 'How many circles can you draw and colour?'
- 'How many hops/skips can you do?'
- 'Talk for one minute about your favourite game, sweet, fruit, etc.'

4 Records

Make worksheets for the children to record what has been done in one minute.

> Name Sandra
> In one minute
> I walked 10 times around the room
> I filled in 3 crosses
> I drew 24 triangles

Ma 2/3d 1/3b
T/B

Measure, Shape and Handling data Workbook **Page 2** *Time: concept of a minute*

In Question 1, the crosses should be drawn from corner to corner of each square, i.e.

 and not ⊠.

In Question 2, the children should write consecutive numbers as indicated.

MINUTES PAST THE HOUR: DIGITAL DISPLAYS
Introductory activities

Ma 2/3e 1/3b 3/3a
T/B3

1 Counting time

Point out to the children that there are four windows or spaces for numbers on a digital clock. The two on the left of the dots are where the *hours* are counted (10 o'clock).

$$10:00$$

The two on the right of the dots are where the *minutes* are counted. Let the children watch the minutes being counted.

'1 minute past 10'   '2 minutes past 10'   '3 minutes past 10'

134

Discuss what happens near the next hour.

Emphasise the reason for this, namely that there are 60 minutes in 1 hour.

You could prepare a card for your display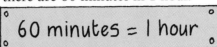

60 minutes = 1 hour

2 What time is it?

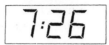

Show the children how to read digital times such as

Many are likely to read this as 'seven twenty-six'. To emphasise the meaning, encourage the children to say 'twenty-six minutes after seven o'clock' or 'twenty-six minutes past seven' at this stage.

The digital time which was read previously by the children as 'half past ten' could now also be read as '30 minutes past 10'.

Care must be taken to ensure that times like | 11:03 | and | 11:30 | are not confused.

3 Sequences

Ask the children to complete sequences of times in which the times increase or decrease in one-minute intervals.

1:07	1:08	1:09	____	____	____
11:57	11:58	11:59	____	____	____
3:20	3:19	3:18	____	____	____

The second of these sequences is particularly important as the hour display changes from one hour to the next.

From sequences, the children could be introduced to the ideas of 'one minute before' and 'one minute after'. Oral questions such as 'What time is one minute before 6 minutes past 10?' could now be asked.

4 Clocks and watches

Many children have digital watches of their own and may also be familiar with the displays on video recorders, car clocks, clock radios, and bus and railway station clocks.

The children should practise reading times on these clocks, putting times in order and interpreting them.

'What time does the train leave?'

'What time does the train arrive?'

'If you arrived at the station at 20 minutes past 10, would you catch the train?'

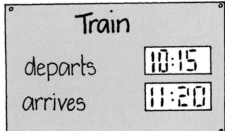

Train
departs 10:15
arrives 11:20

5 Journeys and times

Discuss a journey and insert the times at the various points.

'When did we stop for lunch?'

'At half past 10, where were we?'

'Had we arrived at the library by 10 minutes past 2?'

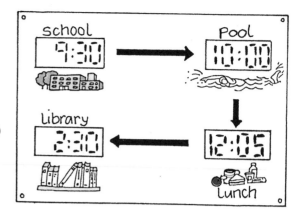

Ma 2/3e 1/3b 3/3a
T/B3 PSE

Problem solving

Measure, Shape and Handling data Workbook **Pages 3 and 4** *Time: digital times*

On Page 3, the children have to complete a sequence, in minutes, of digital times as the child proceeds to the railway station. To give further practice in saying digital times, the children could be asked to read the times in both Questions 1 and 2 when these are completed.

The digital times on Page 4 are to be interpreted as following each other sequentially in the same afternoon. For Question 3, the children must be able to relate the time '10 minutes past 4' to the sequence of events.

MINUTES PAST THE HOUR: ANALOGUE DISPLAYS
Introductory activities

Ma 1/3b 2/3e 3/3a
T/B2

In this section the children relate the minute interval to the analogue clock display. Ideally, a real working clock, clearly marked in minutes, would be best for this purpose since the children could see the minute hand pass through the minute divisions. You may wish to demonstrate on a model clock where the hour hand has been removed or on an hour-timer similar to that shown on Measure, Shape and Handling data Workbook, Page 5.

1 The minute hand

■ Demonstrate that, as the long hand moves round, it passes through minutes of time, which are indicated on the clockface. Starting from the o'clock position (12) the minutes could be counted as the hand sweeps round the clockface:

'one, two, three, four, *five*'

'six, seven, eight, nine, *ten*'

The children should soon realise that the counting is more easily done in *fives*.

'five, ten, fifteen, *twenty*'

Give the children practice in counting round in fives for such positions as

'five, ten, ... *twenty-five*'   and   'five, ten, fifteen, ... *forty*'

■ Discuss times where the number of minutes is not a multiple of five and show that the same technique of counting in fives is used, for example, 'five, ten, fifteen ... thirty-five, thirty-six, *thirty-seven*'.

2 The hour hand

Although the emphasis is on counting minutes on the clockface, remind or show the children that, as the minute hand makes one complete sweep, the hour hand has moved from one number to the next. This is especially important in recording the time when the minute hand has passed the '6' position.

In the example shown, children could wrongly read this as '55 minutes past 3'.

3 What time is it?

Set the clock to a particular time and ask the children to read the time, and then write the time. At this stage, the children should be taught to use the phrase 'minutes past the hour'. This corresponds to what is shown on a digital display.

'14 minutes past 10'   '43 minutes past 3'

4 Guess the time

It may not always be possible for all the children to read the minute marks accurately since the marks may be indistinct at a distance. Also the clockface may be small. The children could be challenged to guess the time and write it down. The teacher (or a child near the clock) could confirm the exact time.

16 minutes past 1 ?

5 Set the time

On a model clock or a real clock the children could be given a time and asked to set the hands correctly.

18 minutes past 10

42 minutes past 6

6 What happened in one hour?

A diary of events could be kept to record the events for one hour's duration in the classroom.

From 9 o'clock to 10 o'clock

10 minutes past 9	Nurse came in
28 minutes past 9	Peter left room
32 minutes past 9	Stopped reading

Ma 1/3ab 2/3e
T/B2 PSE

Extension

Problem solving

Problem solving

Measure, Shape and Handling data Workbook **Pages 5 to 7**   *Time: analogue times*

The sponsored silence scenario used on Pages 5 and 6 gives the opportunity for children to record the number of minutes past the hour.

Question 3 on Page 5 is flagged 'Extension'.

Question 2 on Page 6 involves problem solving.

On Page 7, the events provide a sequence of times over the afternoon, and these have to be read and then recorded. Further discussion and questions could be worthwhile here, for example,

'When did Mark leave the pool?'
'When did Mark go into the café?'
'Where was he at 4 o'clock?'

Questions such as 'How long did he spend at the pool?' are difficult for children at this stage but answers could be found by counting the minutes round the marked clockface.

Question 2 involves problem solving.

MATCHING DIGITAL AND ANALOGUE TIMES
Introductory activities

Ma 2/3e 1/3b
T/B2,3

1 The same times

The children are now required to relate one time display (digital) to the other time display (analogue).

Show a digital clock and an analogue clock with matching times, for example,

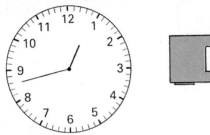

The child should read both times as '43 minutes past 12'.

Give the children an analogue display and ask them to write the equivalent digital time.

Give the children a digital display and ask them to set the hands correctly on an analogue clockface to the corresponding time.

2 Write the times

Use a clockface stamp to make examples as shown.

___ minutes past ___

___ minutes past ___

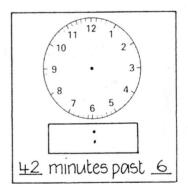

42 minutes past 6

3 Time cards

Make a set of cards each with an analogue time on one side and the equivalent digital time on the other.

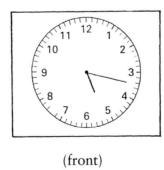

(front)

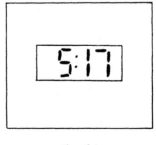

(back)

- A child could pick up a card, write the analogue time as a digital time, and check by turning the card over.

- The set of cards could be positioned with the analogue times uppermost then arranged in order of time. On turning over each card, the digital time sequence would be seen and the correctness of ordering could be checked.

4 Posters

The children could make charts and posters which show analogue and digital displays.

Discussion and questions should arise from such charts, for example,

'What time are the letters collected?'

'If you posted a letter at 49 minutes past 4, would it be collected that day?'

'Would you get into the pool at 2 minutes past 8?'

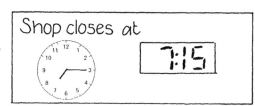

Ma 2/3e
T/B2,3

> ### Textbook Page 27 *Time: matching times*
>
> When writing the digital times in Question 1, the children could draw 'rectangular enclosing frames' or simply write the numerals, for example, 9:10.

QUARTER PAST AND QUARTER TO
Introductory activities

Ma 2/3e 1/3b
T/B2,3

1 Quarter past and quarter to

The phrase 'half past', introduced in Heinemann Mathematics 2, describes the time when the minute hand on an analogue clockface is *half-way* round the dial. At half past, the minute hand points to 6 and the children can now also read this time as '30 minutes past'.

■ Show the children that when the minute hand is *quarter way* round the dial (pointing to 3) the phrase *quarter past* can be used. A clockface shaded in quarters may help the children to understand.

'15 minutes past 1' can now be read as *'quarter past 1'*.

The equivalent digital display is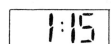

■ Similarly when the minute hand has still a *quarter way* to go to the next o'clock, the phrase *quarter to* can be used. The emphasis now is on the following hour.

'45 minutes past 1 ' can now be read as '*quarter to 2*'.

The equivalent digital display is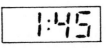

2 Matching games

Make a set of cards, showing equivalent times, for the children to play matching games and activities.

  quarter to 3

Some children might find the phrase 'quarter to' difficult to associate with the other equivalents and so they might require a great deal of practice.

Ma 2/3e
T/B2,3

Textbook Page 28 *Time: quarter past and quarter to*

If the children have understood the introductory activities above they should be able to complete this page fairly easily.

ONE HOUR BEFORE AND AFTER; SIMPLE DURATIONS
Introductory activities

Ma 1/3ab 2/3e
T/B1,2,3,C3

The language 'before' and 'after' was introduced in Heinemann Mathematics 2 in relation to events which were familiar to the children. It is now related to analogue and digital displays where the children tell the times 'one hour before' and 'one hour after' a given time.

Finally the children are asked to calculate the interval of time, in hours, between a starting time and a finishing time.

1 Which comes before? Which comes after?

Flashcards showing familiar sequences of events could be presented to the children.

■ After some discussion questions similar to the following could be asked:

'Which meal comes earliest/latest?' breakfast

'Which meal is before lunch/after lunch?' lunch

'Is lunch before or after tea?' tea

■ Similar questions could be asked for sequences like these:

 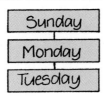 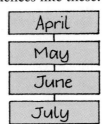

2 Tell the story

Present events out of order and ask the children to make up the correct sequence by considering questions such as

'Did the boy fall off *before* his leg was hurt?'

'Did the doctor come *after* the boy fell off?'

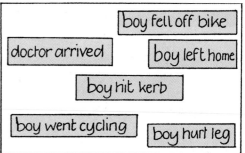

3 One hour before/one hour after

■ Demonstrate, with real or geared clocks, the movement of the hands for *one hour*, starting at the positions of 'o'clock', 'half past', 'quarter past', or 'quarter to'.

By using two clocks, the children could see the starting and finishing times.

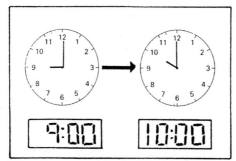 

Since *one hour after* 9 o'clock is seen to be 10 o'clock, the children should realise that *one hour before* 10 o'clock is 9 o'clock.

■ Give the children a time display and then ask them to read and write the times 'one hour before' and 'one hour after':

'What is the time?'

'What was the time one hour before?'

'What will be the time one hour after?'

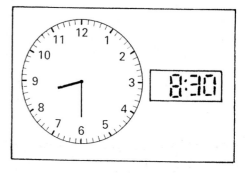

4 Time sequences

Give the children the times of various events and ask them to order them. Ask questions which use the language 'one hour before' and 'one hour after'.

'When is the tiger fed?'
'Who is fed one hour before this?'
'Who is fed one hour after the tiger?'

'When is the penguin fed?'
'Who is fed one hour after this?'

5   How long did it take?

■ Durations of time can be worked out by considering simple journeys and using the idea of 'one hour after'. For example, a chart or worksheet could be produced:

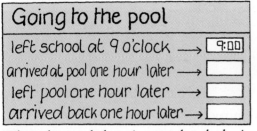

The same journey times could be shown by winding on the hands of an analogue clock.

When the worksheet is completed, the journey is seen to take 3 hours.

■ The children could now work out simple durations, in hours, given the starting and finishing times. They might still need the help of clock displays to count forward the hours, especially if the duration crosses noon.

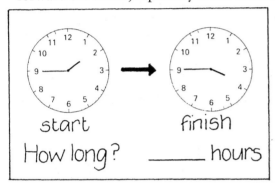

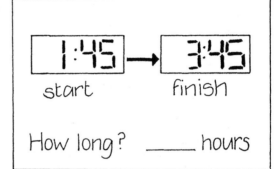

Ma 2/3e
T/B2,3,C3

Textbook Page 29   *Time: duration in hours*

In Questions 1 and 2, the child could be asked to write the times as, for example,

1 (a)   *one hour before*   *now*   *one hour after*
           3 o'clock   4 o'clock   5 o'clock

They should write the 'middle' time first.

Ma 2/3e 5/3a
PS/B2 T/B

Textbook Page 30   *Other activity: interpreting a calendar*

■ Page 30 could be attempted at any time. It is not intended that the children make a detailed study of calendars, since this work will be carried out at a later stage.

■ The purpose of the page is to present a calendar for one month which will promote enquiry and discussion. The children are also asked to carry out a simple investigation using a calendar of their own.

Investigation

■ You could discuss calendars and their purpose before the children attempt Page 30, explaining that the days of the month are numbered 1, 2, 3, . . . and that 3 January, for example, means the third day of January.

Additional activities
Follow-up work could include discussion of

■ months and the seasons

■ important dates and months, for example, Christmas day, class birthdays, school holidays, etc.

Length

Overview

This section

- revises non-standard units
- discusses the need for a standard unit and introduces the metre
- provides practical activities for measuring and estimating lengths in metres and half metres
- introduces the centimetre
- provides practical measuring and estimating activities involving centimetres
- demonstrates the relationship 100 cm ↔ 1 m.

Key words and phrases

spans	measure	tape measure	about 4 metres/centimetres
feet	estimate	how much longer	nearly 3 metres/centimetres
metre	centimetre	how far	a bit more than 5 metres/centimetres
half metre	ruler		3 and a bit metres

Resources

Useful materials

- uncalibrated metre sticks, half metre strips of card

- objects to measure, e.g. ties, belts, card 'fish', snakes', etc

- centimetre cubes and rulers marked in centimetres only

- metre stick calibrated to show 100 cm

- tape measure marked in centimetres (e.g. 150 cm long)

- sheets of sugar paper or card, coloured sticky shapes, sticky tape

- materials suggested for use within the introductory activities

- flashcards of key words and phrases

Assessment and Resources Pack

Assessment

Check-ups

Check-up 2
MSHD Workbook Pages 8–14
(Length m and cm)

Resources

Problem Solving Activities
13 My word (Length words)
14 Joe's height (Measuring in cm)
15 Wagon train (Measuring activity)

Teaching notes

INTRODUCING THE METRE
Introductory activities

Ma 2/2d 1/3b
ME/A1,B1

In Heinemann Mathematics 2 a variety of non-standard units were used to measure lengths. They included rods, feet, paper clips, spans, paces and sticks. (Although the sticks were a metre long, the children were not aware of this.) In this section this work is revised, so that the children appreciate the need for a standard unit.

The metre is then introduced and the children are provided with practical experience of measuring and estimating in metres. Suggestions are given below for practical activities and discussion to introduce this new work.

1 Measuring in feet and spans

■ Revise measuring in 'feet' by asking some children to measure the length of a cupboard or other suitable object. Others could measure the length of a table in spans. Remind the children that they should not leave gaps.

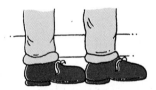

■ Also, revise ways of dealing with the 'bits left over'.

about 4 feet   about 6 spans

Record the results in a table on a large sheet of paper or the chalkboard as they will be helpful in a discussion about the need for a standard unit.

2 The need for a standard unit

Discuss the results of measuring using non-standard units. For example,

	Length of table
Derek	10 spans
Teacher	6 spans
Jason	9 spans

The children should realise that the results are different because the three people have different sizes of hand span. Derek has a *shorter* span than Jason or the teacher and so needs *more* of his spans to match the length of the cupboard.

From the discussion, point out that it would be useful to measure using something which is always the same length and does not vary from one person to another.

3 Introducing the metre

Introduce an uncalibrated metre stick or blank, cardboard metre strip as a length which is always the same length no matter who uses it. Allow the children to measure objects using metre sticks or strips to see if they are longer or shorter than 1 metre. For example, a tie is usually longer than a metre. A belt might be about 1 metre long.

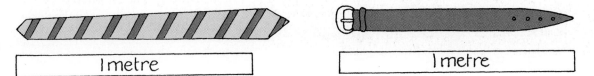

1 metre   1 metre

Children usually find it easy to name objects which are very much longer or shorter than a metre. Experience of measuring objects fairly close to 1 metre long is useful in building up their concept of a metre. It is worthwhile making sure that there are such objects available in the classroom.

Ma 2/2d 1/3b
ME/B1

Measure, Shape and Handling data Workbook **Page 8** *Length: the metre*

Uncalibrated metre sticks or strips should be used for Page 8.

In Question 4, the children should be encouraged to name objects which are not very much longer or shorter than a metre.

When carrying out the investigation in Question 5, the children may need chalk to mark the start of their jumps.

Investigation

MEASURING AND ESTIMATING IN METRES
Introductory activities

1 Measuring techniques

Ma 2/2d 1/3b 2/3d
ME/B1,C4

■ Practical work and discussion should encourage good techniques in measuring using metres. For example, the length of a wall display in the classroom could be measured with *two* metre sticks, used alternatively without leaving gaps.

Such a length could be recorded as 'about 3 metres' with phrases such as 'just over 3 metres' and '3 metres and a bit' being said orally. Fitting the metre stick once again would show that in this case, it is '3 metres and a bit' rather than 'nearly 4 metres'.

Repeat for other lengths stressing this type of language as all the measurements will be approximate.

- One metre stick instead of two should eventually be used for measuring. Two children working together would allow one to make a mark at the end of the stick with a chalk mark or a finger, so that the other one could move the stick to measure the next metre.

2 Estimating

Introduce the idea of estimating each length before measuring. The children may guess wildly at first. This should improve if children are encouraged to visualise how many metre lengths will fit along the length to be estimated.

3 Recording

Introduce the abbreviation m for metres. There should be no capital letter, plural or full stop.

For example 5 metres would be written as 5 m

Ma 2/3d 1/3b 2/2d
ME/B1,3,C4

Measure, Shape and Handling data Workbook   **Page 9**   *Length: estimating and measuring in metres*

The two drawings at the top of Page 9 should be discussed with the children. Make clear that the car's length is 'about 4 metres' as it is just a little more than 4 metres, while its width is 'about 2 metres' although, in fact, it is a little less than 2 metres.

In Question 1, two metre sticks for each pair of children might be required, especially to measure the height of the door. The children should estimate and then measure each object in turn as this might help their estimates to improve from one object to the next.

Question 2 might be attempted using a single metre stick.

MEASURING AND ESTIMATING IN HALF METRES
Introductory activities

Ma 2/2dc 2/3d 1/3b
ME/B1,C4

The concept of 'one half' linked to shapes was introduced in Heinemann Mathematics 2. The notation $\frac{1}{2}$ is introduced in Heinemann Mathematics 3, Workbook 2. Some teachers may wish to complete the work on notation before the children are introduced to the $\frac{1}{2}$ metre.

1 Introducing the half metre

Make strips of card or paper one metre long.

Each child should then fold and cut a strip in half to produce two half metre lengths.

These are then labelled as shown.

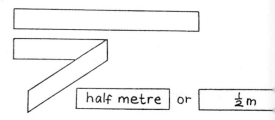

2 Using the half metre

- Ask the children to use their half metre strips to find objects in the classroom which are about one half metre long. These could be listed as shown.

- Ask the children to write down the names of some objects whose lengths they think are

  'a bit' shorter than $\frac{1}{2}$ m
  'a bit' more than $\frac{1}{2}$ m
  more than $\frac{1}{2}$ m but less than 1 m

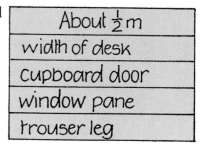

148

3 Measuring and estimating in metres and half metres

The children should now measure lengths using a metre stick and a half metre strip where the measurement in metres only is unsatisfactory due to the 'bit left over'.

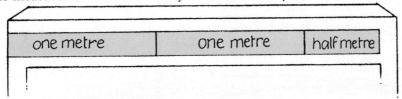

Show that a length of 'about two and one half metres' is recorded as $2\frac{1}{2}$ m.

Some children might now be able to estimate lengths as 'about $1\frac{1}{2}$ m', 'about $2\frac{1}{2}$ m', and so on.

| Measure, Shape and Handling data Workbook **Page 10** *Length: the half metre* |

If the children have already made half metre strips as suggested in the introductory activities, they need not do Question 1.

The form of recording used in Question 4 might have to be re-emphasised since this might be the first time that some children have written mixed numbers.

MEASURING AND ESTIMATING IN CENTIMETRES
Introductory activities

This section need not be attempted immediately after the work on metres.

Practical activities are necessary to introduce the centimetre, either some of those suggested below or similar ones related to thematic work ongoing in the class.

1 Introducing the centimetre

Ask the children to estimate, and then help you to measure, the length in metres of the chalkboard or a card 'python'.

Length of snake

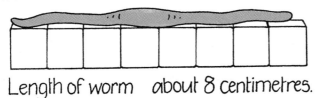

Estimate   about 2 metres.   Measure   about $2\frac{1}{2}$ metres

Introduce a small object, say 8 cm long, such as a pencil or a card 'worm'. Establish that there is no point in measuring it in metres – a metre stick, or even $\frac{1}{2}$ metre, is much too long. Introduce the centimetre as the length of edge of a small cube and fit cubes along the 'worm'.

Length of worm   about 8 centimetres.

At this point the group of children might measure other cardboard 'worms' for themselves, using centimetre cubes.

2   Using a ruler

Discuss the problems of fitting a lot of cubes in a row, for example, keeping the row straight and the time it takes. Some children may suggest using a ruler. Demonstrate that centimetre cubes match the markings on the ruler. Allow the children to help in measuring objects using the ruler. Rulers marked only in centimetres, and where the scale starts at the end of the ruler, are most suitable at first. The abbreviation cm should be introduced.

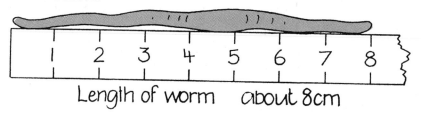

Length of worm   about 8cm

3   Foot lengths

Ask a group of children to draw round one of their feet on paper and cut out the foot shape. They should then measure its length in centimetres. A display of feet in order of size can then be created along a wall.

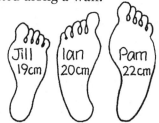

4   Estimating lengths

Discuss particular lengths which could help the children to estimate other lengths in centimetres, for example,

the width of a child's small finger – about 1cm
the length of a Tillich 10 rod – 10 cm
the width of their book – about 21 cm
the length of a ruler – 30 cm

Cardboard fish could be used to give practice in estimating.

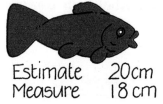

Estimate   20cm
Measure   18 cm

'Is the fish longer or shorter than 10 cm?'
'Estimate its length. How long do you *think* it is?'

Each fish could be compared to the lengths above and to the previous fish to help estimate lengths.

'Is this fish longer or shorter than the first one?'

Measure, Shape and
Handling data
Workbook

Ma 2/3ed 1/3b 2/2b
ME/B1,6,C4

Investigation

When the children measure the width of the page on Page 11, Question 1, it is worth pointing out how difficult it is to fit a lot of cubes together and that it takes a long time. A ruler, marked in centimetres only, is later introduced as it saves time and is more accurate.

When investigating spans on Page 11, Question 4, the children might measure and write down lengths of spans or cut paper strips to match their spans and then measure them before finding the difference in length.

The children should estimate and then measure the length of each fish in turn when attempting Page 12, Question 1, as practical experience should improve their estimations as they go along.

In Question 3, they are asked to draw a fish to a given length. Further work of the kind is suggested on Page 152 of the Teacher's Notes.

CENTIMETRES AND METRES
Introductory activities

1 The relationship 1m ↔ 100 cm
Use a metre stick which is blank on one side and marked in centimetres on the other.

Turn the stick over to show that 1 metre is the same length as 100 cm.

Place a $\frac{1}{2}$ m strip against this to show that $\frac{1}{2}$ m is the same length as 50 cm.

2 Using a metre stick marked in centimetres
Measure 'longer' objects (from 30 to 100 cm) with the children, concentrating on interpreting the scale. For example,

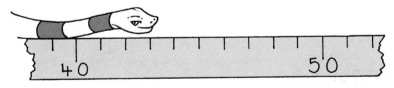

Discuss 'counting on' from 40 and that this length is 'a bit more than 43 cm' or 'about 43 cm'.

3 Estimating
Familiarise the children with the lengths of objects such as a 10 rod (10 cm), a ruler (30 cm), a half metre (50 cm) and a metre stick (100 cm). Provide other objects and discuss estimating their lengths by relating them to the objects described above.

'Is it longer or shorter than $\frac{1}{2}$ metre, . . . 50 cm?'
'Is it more than 30 cm – the length of your ruler?'

4 Using tapes

Ask the children how they would measure the length around their waists. Allow them to show that a metre stick or ruler is of little use. They may suggest the use of string or a paper strip which is then measured with a metre stick marked in cm.

Introduce flexible tapes (for example, 150 cm long preferably marked in cm only) and demonstrate their use with the help of two children. Discuss ways of reading a length from a tape which may overlap itself.

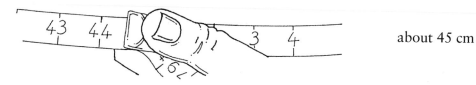

about 45 cm

5 Making a wall display

The children could draw and colour fish, eels, stones, weeds, castles, etc., of a given size, for example, 8cm, $\frac{1}{2}$ metre, etc. These could then contribute to a wall display showing a fish tank with captions about lengths, for example,

The tallest weed measures about 34 cm.

Ma 2/3d 2/3e
ME/B1,6,C4,5

Measure, Shape and Handling data Workbook **Pages 13 and 14** *Length: using a metre stick and a tape*

On Page 13, Question 2, the children might use chalk marks to help them measure stride lengths. The two partners should measure each other. When estimating, they might find it helpful to think of familiar lengths - a ruler: 30 cm, a half metre: 50 cm – and judge other objects as longer or shorter than this.

In Questions 3 and 4, the rectangle made from six maths books should measure about 63 cm by 60 cm; the row of four books about 84 cm.

All of the measurements on Page 14 could be found using a tape although in some cases (e.g. 'lift your knee') a non-flexible metre stick might be better. All of the sizes should be less than 100 cm for children at this stage.

Ma 2/3e 1/3ab
ME/B1,6

Textbook Page 31 *Length: practical work*

The aim of this activity is for the children to measure in centimetres, using a tape, in order to create a waistcoat which is neither too tight nor too loose and can be worn without falling apart.

Discuss with the children the purpose of the activity, and possible ways of working.

You will need large sheets of coloured 'sugar' or similar paper, sticky tape for joining, and coloured sticky shapes.

Area

Measure, Shape and
Handling data
Workbook

Ma 1/3ab
Ma 2/2d
ME/A1,2,4,C7

Overview

This section

- compares the areas of shapes, drawn on squared grids, by counting squares
- deals with drawing shapes with specified areas on squared grids
- introduces the idea of conservation of area.

	Teacher's Notes	Measure, Shape and Handling data Workbook	Textbook
Finding and comparing areas by counting squares	154	15, 16	32

Key words and phrases

| area | greater area | square(s) | half |
| same area | smaller area | | whole |

Resources

Useful materials

- squared paper (1 cm, 2 cm or 5 cm)
- coloured pencils or crayons
- rulers
- other materials suggested within the introductory activities
- flashcards of key words and phrases

Assessment and Resources Pack

Assessment

Check-ups

Check-up 3
MSHD Workbook Pages 15–18
(Area and volume)

Teaching notes

FINDING AND COMPARING AREAS BY COUNTING SQUARES
Introductory activities

Ma 2/2d 1/3b
ME/A1,2,4,C7

The concept of area and measuring areas using non-standard units were introduced in Heinemann Mathematics 2.

In this section areas are measured and compared by counting squares. The square centimetre will be introduced in Heinemann Mathematics 4.

1 Revision

■ Remind the children of what is meant by the area of a shape, i.e. the amount of surface it has.

■ Ask the children to compare the areas of two shapes by covering each with squares and counting them.

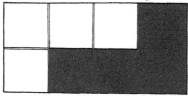

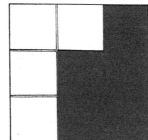

area is ____ squares

area is ____ squares

2 Using squared paper

■ Ask the children to draw shapes on squared paper and find their area by counting squares.

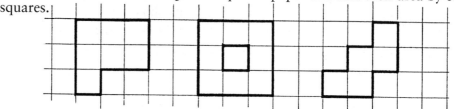

area is 7 squares   area is 8 squares   area is 5 squares

■ Ask the children to draw, on squared paper, shapes having specified areas, for example 10 squares.

3 Comparing areas

Stick a piece of squared paper on to card, draw a set of shapes and cut them out.

Present these blank side up to the children and ask

‘Which shape has the largest area?’

‘Which shape has the smallest area?’

The shapes are then turned over and the squares are counted to check.

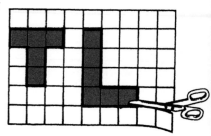

154

4 Shapes with the same area

Use 2 cm squared paper. Ask the children to draw different shapes each of which has an area of, for example, 5 squares. These could be cut out and displayed as a poster.

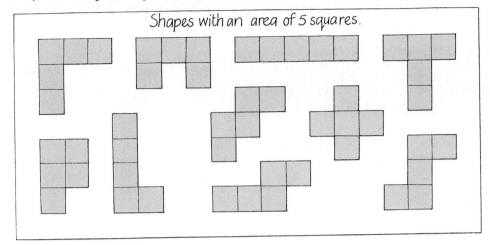

Shapes with an area of 5 squares.

Repeat for other numbers of squares.

Ma 2/2d 1/3b
ME/A1,2,4,C7

Measure, Shape and Handling data Workbook   **Pages 15 and 16**   *Area: counting squares and comparing areas*

After completing Page 15, Question 1, the children could be asked to draw other letters of the alphabet on squared paper, and to find their areas by counting squares.

Question 3 involves the idea of conservation of area.

On Page 16, Question 1, a child could draw either a larger shape and then count the squares to find its area, or count the squares on the original shape and then make a shape with a greater number of squares. Similar procedures could be used to draw a shape smaller than the given one. Although a limited amount of grid is available for the two new shapes the fact that the larger shape has to be drawn first should mean that no difficulty should be experienced in accommodating the smaller shape, which could be as small as one square.

In Question 2, the children should answer the question by using visual perception, before counting the squares.

Ma 2/2d 1/3a
ME/A1,4

Textbook Page 32   *Area: counting squares*

In Question 1, all the aliens have the same area.

The aliens made in Question 3 could be cut out, coloured and displayed.

Volume

Overview

This section

■ discusses the need for a standard unit and introduces the litre

■ gives the children experience in estimating and measuring in litres.

	Teacher's Notes	Measure, Shape and Handling data Workbook	Textbook
Introducing the litre	157	17, 18	
Problem solving		17, 18	

Key words and phrases

volume   capacity   container   measure   estimate   litre

Resources

Useful materials

■ commercial litre measure

■ containers which hold about 2, 3 and 4 litres

■ containers with the symbol 'e' on them

■ paper cups and a kettle

■ other materials suggested within the introductory activities

■ flashcards of key words and phrases

Assessment and Resources Pack

Assessment

Check-ups

Check-up 3
MSHD Workbook Pages 15–18
(Area and volume)

Resources

Problem Solving Activities
16 Pour it out (Halving a volume)

INTRODUCING THE LITRE
Introductory activities

Measuring with non-standard units of capacity and volume was introduced in
Heinemann Mathematics 2.

Ma 2/2d 1/3b 2/3d
ME/A1,4,C2

In this section the children are introduced to the litre.

It is essential that they have practical experience of estimating and measuring before
they try the workbook pages. A class collection of containers which children might
see in the supermarket or at home would be very useful for the work on these pages.

1 The need for a standard unit

Ask the children to use a breakfast cup to find the capacity of a large container.
Repeat the activity using a teacup and a coffee cup.

They should obtain different results, for example,

about two breakfast cups
about three teacups
about five coffee cups

Ask the children to explain why their answers are different. They should be able to
comment that the cups used have different capacities.

This should lead to the need for a standard unit and hence to the introduction of the
litre. Show the children a commercial measure marked 1 litre.

2 Using a litre

Ask the children to find, from the class collection, differently shaped containers
which they think might hold

■ about one litre

■ more than one litre

■ less than one litre

Use the litre measure to check. The
containers could be displayed as shown.

3 Making a collection

Ask the children to bring from home empty containers which hold about one litre.
Discuss how varied the shapes of these containers are and ask the children to check
whether they each hold 'about 1 litre', 'more than 1 litre' or 'less than 1 litre'. These
containers could be added to the display.

4 Measuring and estimating in litres

Ask the children to use a litre measure to find the capacity of several large
containers, for example, a mixing bowl, a soup pot, a bucket or a large vase. A
container with a capacity of, for example, 'just under' or 'just over' 2 litres should be
recorded as having a capacity of 'about 2 litres'.

Measure, Shape and
Handling data Workbook   **Pages 17 and 18**   *Volume: litres*

For Page 17, Question 1, provide a set of containers similar to those illustrated.

Children who have difficulty with Question 2 might have to do it practically.

Two or three items could be acceptable for the list in Question 3. The children could look for the 'e' symbol on containers and packets. This indicates that the volume measure is one accepted throughout the EEC countries.

For Page 18, Question 1, the children are expected to use their results from the first two parts of the question to answer the last part. This answer could then be checked using a litre measure.

Weight

Overview

This section

■ discusses the need for a standard unit of weight

■ introduces the kilogram, the half kilogram and the abbreviation 'kg'

■ provides estimating and weighing activities using these weights.

	Teacher's Notes	Measure, Shape and Handling data Workbook	Textbook
Introducing the kilogram	160	19	
Introducing the half kilogram	161	20	33
The kilogram Additional activities	162		

Key words and phrases

one kilogram   weighs more than/less than/about one kilogram   estimate
half a kilogram   weighs more than/less than/about half a kilogram   two-pan balance

Resources

Useful materials

■ two-pan balances, cubes, marbles, sand, Plasticine

■ kilogram and half kilogram weights

■ prepared packets, tins, etc., for weighing (see Pages 160 and 161)

■ other materials suggested within the introductory and additional activities

■ flashcards of key words and phrases

Assessment and Resources Pack

Assessment	Resources
Check-ups	*Problem Solving Activities*
Check-up 4 MSHD Workbook Pages 19, 20 (Weight and choosing units)	17 Balancing act (Using a two-pan balance)

Teaching notes

INTRODUCING THE KILOGRAM (1 kg)
Introductory activities

Ma 2/2d 1/3b 2/3d
ME/A1,B2

Weighing using non-standard units and a two-pan balance was introduced in Heinemann Mathematics 2. Language used included 'heavier', 'lighter', 'weighs more/less', 'heaviest', 'lightest', 'weighs about' and 'balances'.

This section introduces the standard unit of one kilogram, its abbreviation 'kg' and the half kilogram. Emphasis is placed on estimating before measuring.

1 The need for a standard unit

Ask the children to weigh an object using marbles. Give them round beads of a comparable size to the marbles and ask them to weigh the object again. Discuss why the results are different.

A marble is heavier than a bead and so fewer marbles are required than beads to weigh the object.

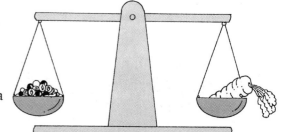

Point out that if we want to weigh and compare weights of different objects then a 'standard' unit of weight is required.

2 Introducing the kilogram (1 kg)

Introduce the word 'kilogram' by discussing buying potatoes, sugar, etc. Pass round a packet of sugar and a commercial 1 kg weight for each child to hold. Introduce the abbreviation 'kg', from examination of the kilogram weight or a packet of sugar. (Note that a lower case 'k' is used and there is no full stop after kg unless at the end of a sentence.)

3 Using the 1 kg weight

■ Ask the children to use a two-pan balance and a 1 kg weight to weigh out 1 kg of sand. The sand should then be placed in a polythene bag and labelled '1 kg'.

■ Ask the children to weigh out *about* 1 kg of potatoes, 1 kg of apples, etc. Take care to choose a commodity which will fit the available two-pan balance.

■ A plastic shopping bag could be packed with items so that the total weight is *about* 1 kilogram.

4 Estimating and weighing

The children should have experience of estimating and weighing objects to find if a weight is 'more than', 'less than' or 'about' 1 kilogram. Alternative language, such as 'heavier than', 'lighter than' and 'about the same weight as' should also be used.

Find or prepare a selection of items suitable for a two-pan balance, for example,

a stone wrapped in paper
small stones or sand sealed in a packet or tin
plastic shopping bags with items in them
carrots, potatoes, etc., in plastic bags.

Ask the children to estimate, then weigh each item in turn and place it beside the appropriate label.

Show them how to estimate either by holding the 1 kg weight in one hand and the item in the other or using both hands to hold the item first and then the kilogram weight. The estimate should then be checked using a two-pan balance.

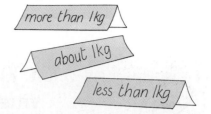

Measure, Shape and Handling data Workbook **Page 19** *Weight: the kilogram*

For Questions 1 to 3 items prepared as suggested in Activity 4 above are required. For ease of recording they could be colour-coded or have labels with

| carrots | | sweets | etc. attached to them.

In Question 2, some children might need to show how a 'wrong' estimate could be corrected by scoring or rubbing out the name and entering it on the correct shelf.

Question 5 is a group activity.

The kilogram of Plasticine is required for work on Measure, Shape and Handling data Workbook, Page 20.

INTRODUCING THE HALF KILOGRAM ($\frac{1}{2}$ kg)
Introductory activities

The concept of 'one half' linked to shapes was introduced in Heinemann Mathematics 2. The notation $\frac{1}{2}$ is introduced in Heinemann Mathematics 3, Workbook 2. You might wish the children to complete the work on notation before introducing them to the $\frac{1}{2}$ kg.

1   Introducing the half kilogram ($\frac{1}{2}$ kg)

The children, with supervision, could make half kilogram weights by

- dividing the sand from a 1 kg bag into two equally balanced bags

- halving a kilogram of Plasticine and checking that the two halves 'balance' on the two-pan scales. You could also cover a commercial 500 g weight with a '$\frac{1}{2}$ kg' label.

It is important to link the notation '$\frac{1}{2}$ kg' with the language 'half a kilogram' or 'half of one kilogram'.

2   Using the $\frac{1}{2}$ kg weight

The activities for using the 1 kg weight outlined on Page 160 could be adapted for the $\frac{1}{2}$ kg weight.

3   Estimating and weighing

The children should be involved in estimating and weighing objects to find if a weight is 'more than', 'less than' or 'about' $\frac{1}{2}$ kilogram. Alternative language such as 'heavier than', 'lighter than', 'about the same weight as' should also be used. The items will have to be carefully selected or prepared as outlined for similar work involving the kilogram on Page 160.

Measure, Shape and Handling data Workbook **Page 20** *Weight: the half kilogram*

Question 1 could be omitted if the children have carried out the appropriate part of Activity 1 above.

Textbook Page 33 *Weight: comparison*

Page 33 could act as a check-up on the practical work on Measure, Shape and Handling data Workbook, Pages 19 and 20.

In Question 1, make sure the children understand what sort of 'story' they have to write. In Question 1(f), you should indicate that $1\frac{1}{2}$ kg is read as 'one and a half kilograms' and that it means $1 \text{ kg} + \frac{1}{2}\text{kg}$.

In Question 2, the children have to know that, for example, 1 kg, 1 kg, $\frac{1}{2}$ kg is written as $2\frac{1}{2}$ kg. Similar work is done in the Length section with lengths such as $2\frac{1}{2}$ metres.

THE KILOGRAM
Additional activities

1 Labels on packages

Children could collect labels or packages showing the word 'kilogram' or 'kg'. These could be displayed on a chart.

2 New-born babies

Typical weights of new-born babies could be discussed and illustrated, perhaps, with photographs.

3 Weights of animals

Children could find out and collect information about the weights of animals in kilograms. This information could be displayed on a chart and/or displayed graphically.

 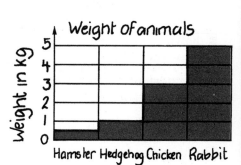

4 Weight of fruit and vegetables

The *Guinness Book of Records* could be consulted to give record-breaking weights of apples, carrots, grapefruit, onions, potatoes, and so on. The weights could be displayed as above on a chart and/or displayed graphically.

Measure

Overview

This section

- deals with choosing appropriate measure units for everyday objects
- provides some measure investigations.

Ma 1/3abd
Ma 2/2d
Ma 2/3e
ME/A1,B1,2,C2,5
T/B
PSE

	Teacher's Notes	Measure, Shape and Handling data Workbook	Textbook
Choosing units and investigations	164		34, 35
Investigation			*35*

Key words and phrases

choose   label   the best measure   about how many

Resources

Useful materials

- materials required for the investigations on Textbook Page 35 – various measuring devices should be made available to the children, for example, metre sticks, tape measure, 1 litre measure, 1 kg and $\frac{1}{2}$ kg weights, timer or watch; saucers, apples
- other materials suggested within the introductory activities
- flashcards of key words and phrases

Assessment and Resources Pack

Assessment

Check-ups

Check-up 4
MSHD Workbook Pages 19–20
(Weight and choosing units)

Teaching notes

CHOOSING UNITS AND INVESTIGATIONS
Introductory activities

This small section could be attempted any time after the work on length, weight and volume has been completed. It contains examples and practical activities involving a variety of measures.

1 Choosing an appropriate unit
Discuss with the children the appropriate measure units used when buying or selling everyday objects. For example, sugar is sold in kilograms, lemonade is sold in litres and so on.

Discuss also the appropriate quantities in which certain commodities are sold. For example, potatoes are sold in 3 kg and 5 kg bags, lemonade is sold in 1 litre, $1\frac{1}{2}$ litre and 2 litre bottles.

2 Investigations
Carry out one or two investigations to introduce the type of work which appears on Textbook Page 35. For example, tell the children

'There was once a street 49 cm wide. Place some desks 49 cm apart and try to walk between them.'

This could be followed up by consulting record books, for example, the *Guinness Book of Records* to find the narrowest street in Britain or in the world.

Textbook Pages 34 and 35 *Choosing units and investigations*

On Page 34, Question 1 contains six labels, two each for length, weight and volume. The answers should be recorded like this

    Potatoes – 3 kg
    Lemonade – 2 litres

and so on.

Question 2 might cause difficulty as it is still quite common to quote a baby's weight in pounds.

Page 35 contains four practical problems which can be attempted in any order. The children could work in pairs and be allocated tasks to make most efficient use of available material. Not all children need do all tasks. Answers could be illustrated on a wall chart with captions attached. Encourage the children to talk about how they found particular answers.

SHAPE

This section contains four separate units dealing with various aspects of shape.
Details of the content, resources and language for each unit are given at the start of
the notes for that unit.

165

3D shape

Overview

This section

■ introduces the triangular prism

■ deals with faces, edges and corners of shapes.

	Teacher's Notes	Measure, Shape and Handling data Workbook	Textbook
Introducing the triangular prism	167	21	
Faces of 3D shapes	168	22	
Edges of 3D shapes	169	23	
Corners of 3D shapes	170	24	
Problem solving		23	

Key words and phrases

face	flat	cube	sphere	triangular prism
edge	curved	cuboid	cylinder	pyramid
corner	straight	cone		

Resources

Useful materials

■ sets of shapes each set having cylinders, cones, cuboids, cubes, spheres, pyramids and triangular prisms

■ cheese portion

■ other materials suggested within the introductory activities

■ flashcards of key words and phrases

Assessment and Resources Pack

Assessment

Check-ups

Check-up 5
MSHD Workbook Pages 21–24
(3D shapes – faces, edges, corners)

Resources

Problem Solving Activities

18 Cubed (Using cubes)
19 Shape kit (Corners and edges of 3D shapes

Resource Cards

Resource Cards 29 to 31 (Name that shape) involve the language of corners, faces and edges.

Teaching notes

INTRODUCING THE TRIANGULAR PRISM
Introductory activities

The children were introduced to the cube, cuboid, cylinder, cone, sphere and square-based pyramid in Heinemann Mathematics 1 and 2. In this unit, shapes already met are revised and the triangular prism is introduced.

Ma 1/3b 4/2a
RS/A2,B2

1 Shape names

Show the children a set of shapes and a set of labels, each with the name of a shape.

Ask the children to match labels to the appropriate shapes. This might be carried out in either of these ways:

- give each child a label and ask him/her to find an appropriate shape
- give each child a 3D shape and ask him/her to find an appropriate label

The children should talk about the shapes as they handle and name them, for example,

  'This is a ball. It's proper name is a sphere.'

The result of the matching could be a display like this:

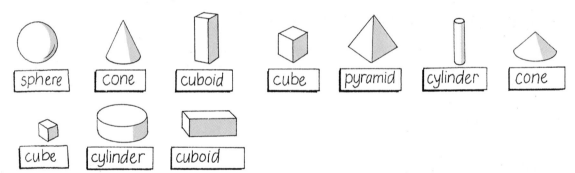

2 A 'new' shape

Add a triangular prism to the display.

Ask the children to describe the shape in their own words. Tell them its correct name – triangular prism.

Show the children how the new shape looks in different positions.

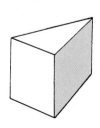  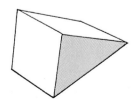

3 Building a tower using triangles

Build up a tower using identical plastic triangles.

Ask the children to name the shape of the tower.

4 The missing shape   *(game)*

On a tray put a set of shapes. There should be one of each shape including a triangular prism.

Ask the children to close their eyes while one shape is removed. Ask them to look at the tray and name the missing shape.

Ma 1/3b 4/2a
RS/A2,B2

Measure, Shape and Handling data Workbook   **Page 21**   *3D shape: triangular prism*

In Question 1, the children should colour cones, cylinders, cuboids and the 'other shapes' according to the colour code indicated. The drawings of shapes could be ticked with the appropriate colour rather than colouring. From the introductory activities, the children should recognise the 'yellow shapes' as triangular prisms.

FACES OF 3D SHAPES
Introductory activities

1 Flat and curved faces

Discuss the faces of 3D shapes and help the children to realise that faces are either flat or curved.

Ma 4/2a 4/3a 1/3b
RS/B1,2

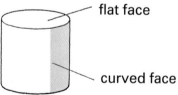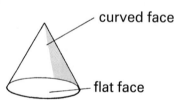

2 Sorting by faces

Ask the children to sort shapes into

- those with only flat faces and 'others'

only flat faces   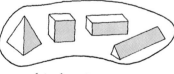   others

- those with a curved face and 'others'

a curved face      others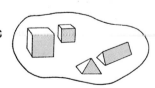

- those with both flat and curved faces and 'others'

both flat and curved faces   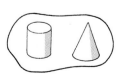   others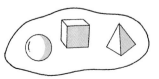

168

3 Number of faces

- Ask the children to label each shape with the number of faces it has.

- Ask the children to short shapes according to the number of faces they have.
  For example, 'shapes with less than 5 faces' and 'others'.

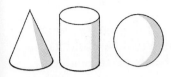   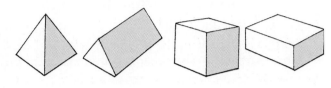

less than 5 faces   others

Measure, Shape and
Handling data Workbook   **Page 22**   *3D shape: faces*

Provide a set of shapes as shown at the top of Page 22. These shapes will also be
required for Pages 23 and 24.

The children should select a shape to match each illustration in Questions 1 to 3
and use the shape to feel and count the faces as appropriate.

In Question 4, after a group has sorted the shapes, another group could be
invited to say how the shapes had been sorted.

EDGES OF 3D SHAPES
Introductory activities

1 Straight or curved edges

Show the children that faces meet at edges and that edges can be straight or curved.

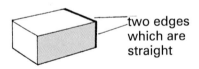   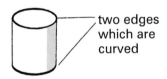

2 Ordering by the number of edges

Ask the children to find a shape with no edges (sphere), a shape with one edge
(cone), and a shape with two edges (cylinder).

3 A challenge

Some more able children could be challenged to use Plasticine to make a shape with
three edges, for example, the segments of a 'chocolate orange'.

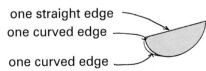

4 Number of edges

Ask the children to find how many edges a cube, a pyramid, a cuboid and a
triangular prism each have. A child could mark each edge with chalk as it is counted.

The set of shapes used on Page 22 is required for this page.

Question 3 could be regarded as problem solving if the children have not attempted this type of question before.

For Question 4 provide an opaque cloth or plastic bag containing shapes. One child feels a shape in the bag and names it. The shape is then removed and its name confirmed. The other children take it in turns to feel a shape and name it.

CORNERS OF 3D SHAPES
Introductory activities

1 Identifying corners
Show the children that edges meet at corners.

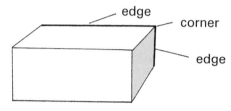

2 Number of corners
Ask the children to find

- two shapes with no corners (sphere, cylinder)

- one shape with one corner (cone)

- one shape with five corners (square based pyramid)

- one shape with six corners (triangular prism)

- two shapes with eight corners (cube, cuboid)

3 Bag game
The children could play the game described above for Measure, Shape and Handling data Workbook, Page 23, Question 4. Feeling the corners could help them to name the shape.

The set of shapes used on Page 22, is again required for this page.

Question 2 investigates the number of faces, edges and corners for different cuboids. This is repeated for cones, cylinders and cubes.

Tiling

Overview

This section introduces children to tiling using squares, rectangles and regular hexagons.

	Teacher's Notes	Measure, Shape and Handling data Workbook	Textbook
Tiling	172	25, 26	
Additional activity	174		

Key words and phrases

tiles   tiling   square   rectangle   hexagon   pattern

Resources

Useful materials

- plastic or cardboard squares, rectangles, regular hexagons
- coloured pencils
- squared paper, triangular dotted paper
- gummed squares, rectangles, regular hexagons
- other materials suggested within the introductory activities
- flashcards of key words and phrases

Assessment and Resources Pack

Assessment

Check-ups

Check-up 6
MSHD Workbook Pages 25–29
(Tiling, right angles, turning)

Teaching notes

TILING
Introductory activities

Ma 4/2a 1/3b
RS/B3

Squares, rectangles, circles, triangles, pentagons and hexagons were introduced in Heinemann Mathematics 1 and 2. This section introduces the children to tiling patterns using squares, rectangles and regular hexagons.

1 Fitting together

Provide the children with a set of congruent plastic or cardboard circles.

Ask them to try fitting them together.

'Are there any gaps?' (*Yes*)

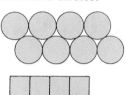

Repeat for congruent squares and rectangles.

'Are there any gaps?' (*No*)

'Squares and rectangles tile. Circles do not tile.'

2 The house

The tiling work on Measure, Shape and Handling data Workbook, Pages 25 and 26 is set within the context of a house.

Give each group of children a large outline of a house as shown.

Discuss features of houses which might exhibit tiling, for example, roofs, walls and paths. The house outlines are used for the activities which follow.

3 Wall patterns using squares

Look at walls in and around the school or photographs of walls and discuss with the children the different types of patterns they see.

Give the children plastic or cardboard squares to create their own wall patterns.

Ask the children then to record their patterns on the house wall either by

■ using gummed squares

or

■ drawing round squares

Patterns could also be recorded by colouring squares on squared paper. These could then be cut out and stuck on to the house wall.

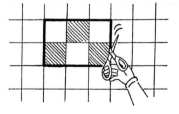

4 Wall patterns using rectangles

Give the children plastic or cardboard rectangles to create another range of tiling

patterns such as

These patterns could be recorded on the house wall as
before.

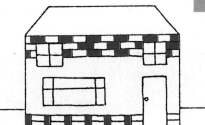

5 Patio patterns using squares and rectangles

Give the children sets of squares and rectangles to explore a variety of patterns for
the patio. Ask the children to record these patterns on squared paper.

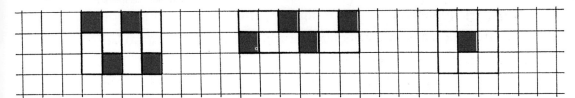

6 Path patterns using regular hexagons

Give the children plastic or cardboard congruent regular hexagons.

Ask them to find out if they tile. The resulting pattern could be recorded by using
triangular dotted paper, drawing round the hexagons or by using coloured gummed
shapes. Add the path to the front of the house.

Ma 4/2a 1/3b
RS/B3

**Measure, Shape and
Handling data Workbook** **Pages 25 and 26**   *Tiling*

Pages 25 and 26 provide a useful way of assessing the children's understanding
of tiling with squares, rectangles and regular hexagons, carried out in the
introductory activities.

On Page 25, Question 1, the brick patterns completed by the children should
match the patterns shown in the illustration of the house.

A room in the house

The children could be asked to design the floor covering, wallpaper and curtain patterns for one room in the house, for example, bedroom, bathroom and so on.

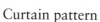

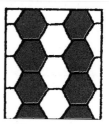

Curtain pattern   Wallpaper pattern   Floor pattern

These patterns could be printed on fabric or paper.

Right angles

Ma 4/2ab
Ma 4/3a
Ma 5/2a
AS/A1
PM/B1,C2
A/B1
C/B1
D/B1
RS/A3,B1
PSE

Overview

This section revises and extends work on

- turning through right angles
- right angles in 2D shapes.

	Teacher's Notes	Measure, Shape and Handling data Workbook	Textbook
Turning through right angles	176	27, 28	
Right angles in 2D shapes	178	29	
Sorting 2D shapes	179		36
Other activities			37, 38
Problem solving			37, 38

Key words and phrases

turn right	turn left	forward	Carroll diagram
directions	right angle	right angle tester	tree diagram

~~right~~ angles This notation is used in a Carroll diagram to mean 'does not have any right angles'.

Resources

Useful materials

- paper circles or scraps of paper for making right angle testers
- 9-pin nailboards, elastic bands
- selection of 2D shapes to test for right angles
- other materials suggested within the introductory activities
- flashcards of key words and phrases

Assessment and Resources Pack

Assessment

Check-ups

Check-up 6
MSHD Workbook Pages 25–29
(Tiling, right angles, turning)

Resources

Problem Solving Activities

20 Rough river journey (Turning through right angles; position and movement)
21 Dotting about (Turning through right angles; position and movement)

Resource Cards

Resource Cards 32 to 34 (Adventure World) involve position and movement, and turning through right angles.

Teaching notes

TURNING THROUGH RIGHT ANGLES
Introductory activities

Ma 4/1b 4/2b 1/3b
PM/B1,C2

In Heinemann Mathematics 2, the children followed instructions for turning right and left, moving forward and back.

1 Turning to the right and left

Although the children have met these terms in Heinemann Mathematics 2, some revision would be worthwhile.

■ Discuss phrases like 'on your right/left' to ensure that children have a full understanding of them.

In the work which follows turn right/left means turn through a right angle to the right/left. It should be emphasised that the turn takes place 'on the spot' and there is no forward movement while turning.

■ It could be revealing to note the outcome of the following:
Give instructions: 'Stand up. Face me. Close your eyes. Turn right. Open your eyes.'

■ Ask two children to stand with their backs to the class as shown. Ask them to turn to face each other. Ask the class

'Who turned right?'
'Who turned left?'

2 Go walkabout

Instructions should now involve moving forward and back as well as turning right and left.

Use a large area, perhaps with floor tiles or a grid marked in chalk, to allow the children to practise moving to instructions such as

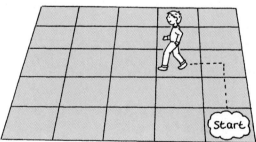

Forward 2
Turn left
Forward 3
Back 1

3 Moving on a grid

This activity introduces movement from dot to dot rather than from square to square.

Make a large grid with objects drawn on it as shown. Provide a counter with an arrow on it to move across the grid.

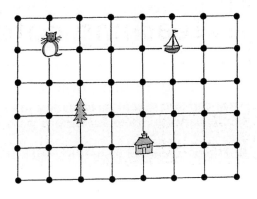

■ Ask a child to give directions to go from the house to the cat. For example, forward 3, turn left, forward 3.

■ Show the abbreviated form of writing this, F3, L, F3.

■ Ask the children to describe different ways of getting from one object to another. For example, from the tree to the house. One possibility is F2, R, F1.

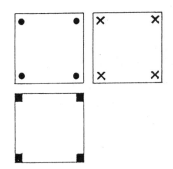

Emphasise that the arrowhead on the counter shows the forward direction.

■ Give a starting point, the direction of the arrowhead and a set of instructions in abbreviated form and ask the child to find the finishing position.

Children should be given much practice in this type of work.

4 Marking right angles

In Heinemann Mathematics 2, right angles were marked by putting a dot or a cross in the appropriate corner. They should now be marked using the more conventional square as shown.

Ma 4/1b 4/2b
PM/B1,C2

Measure, Shape and Handling data Workbook **Pages 27 and 28** *Right angles and turning*

The map on Page 28 is used in conjunction with Page 27. To assist the children with these pages the following suggestions are made.

■ Discuss the map with the children pointing out the various landmarks – snake pit, gold, coloured gates and so on.

■ Give and talk through one or two 'journeys' checking the moves step by step.

■ Make sure that for each starting gate, the children realise which direction they are facing. Some children may need to stand up and face this way, and then turn left or right to follow instructions successfully.

■ Remind children of right angles and how to mark them.

In Question 2, different answers are possible but it is assumed that most children will take the shortest route to the gold.

Because of the large number of instructions required for Questions 5 and 6, the answers should be written in an exercise book. Question 6 gives the children the freedom to go anywhere on the map, for example, from the Wishing Well to the Log Cabin.

RIGHT ANGLES IN 2D SHAPES
Introductory activities

Ma 4/2a 1/3b
A/B1

1 Making a right angle tester

Most children should have made and used a right angle tester in Heinemann Mathematics 2. There are various ways of making one.

- Use the corner of a sheet of paper or card

- Fold a scrap of paper twice as shown

- Fold a paper circle

2 Using a right angle tester

Ask the children to look and test for right angles in the classroom, for example, corners of a desk, a table, a door, a picture and so on.

3 Exploring shapes

- Provide a range of card shapes. Ask the children to use their right angle testers to check for corners which are right angles.

  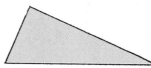

- If shapes like these are drawn on a worksheet the children could test for right angles, and then mark them. Some children might like to test the faces of 3D shapes to see if there are any right angles.

4 Using a nailboard

A simple 9-pin nailboard could be made by pasting a piece of squared paper onto a piece of wood and hammering in 9 nails. The nails should not be less than 2 cm apart, but 3 cm apart will give shapes of a more suitable size.

The corner of a larger nailboard could be used, although this is less satisfactory, particularly for less able children.

Show children how to make shapes with elastic bands on the nailboard and how to test for right angles.

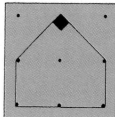

Some children might miss ones such as that shown.

In Question 1, squares and rectangles are relatively easy to make and draw. Encourage children to draw the two rectangles in different orientations. It will be interesting to see if any child finds this square.

In Questions 2 and 3, the children should be encouraged to use the nailboard first. They could then readily correct errors and only when they are convinced that they have a suitable shape, should they transfer it to the workbook page.

Some explanation of 'different' may be necessary in Question 2. Congruent shapes in other positions on the nailboard should not count as 'different'. There are eight completely different triangles, four of which have right angles.

SORTING 2D SHAPES
Introductory activities

1 Carroll diagrams

Children were introduced to Carroll diagrams in Heinemann Mathematics 2.

Sorting children

Revise this form of two-way sorting using a group of children and, for example, the criteria shown.

	boys	not boys
brown eyes	John	Pam Kay
not brown eyes	Peter Eric	Sara

Ask the children to place flashcards of their names in the appropriate compartments.

Once the children are familiar with what has to be done, introduce the new recording convention where ✕ indicates the negative, for example, b⊗ys means *not boys*.

	boys	~~boys~~
brown eyes		
~~brown eyes~~		

Sorting 2D shapes

A selection of shapes could be sorted in different ways and the recording made on a Carroll diagram.

	right angles	~~right angles~~
3 sides		
~~3 sides~~		

2 Tree diagrams

This is a new form of sorting diagram for these children. It involves answering a yes/no question and following the appropriate arrow. A chart similar to the one below would be helpful for the initial explanation.

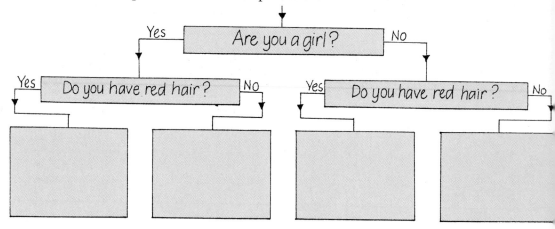

Each child in the group should be taken through the 'tree questions' separately. Flashcards of children's names could be placed in the appropriate boxes.

The questions asked in the diagram could be replaced by others written on cards placed in the appropriate positions. For example,

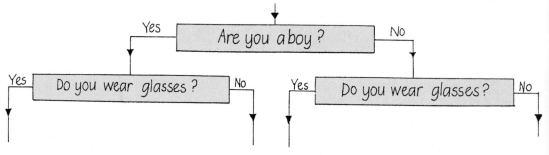

Ma 4/2a 5/2a 4/3a
C/B1 D/B1 RS/B1 A/B1

Textbook Page 36   *Right angles: sorting 2D shapes*

The work on Page 36 gives further practice in sorting shapes using both Carroll and Tree diagrams.

A scenario of place-names on stickers on a suitcase has been used so that the children record the place-name rather than the shape name since some of the shape names might not be known.

The answers to Question 2 should correspond to the sections of the Carroll diagram since the same questions are asked. The shapes shown could be used again and the children asked to sort them in different ways. Different criteria for sorting would have to be chosen, for example, 'Town in Britain' and 'Has exactly 4 sides', or 'Has more than 4 sides' and 'Has right angles', and so on.

Textbook Page 37   *Other activity: domino patterns*

- A set of dominoes is required for Page 37 which could be tackled at any time.

- In Question 1, the children could be asked to investigate other shapes made from 4 dominoes. They could draw round their dominoes to record these shapes.

- In Question 2, the children might match any six dominoes. Some might notice that the domino totals are in sequence – 4, 5, 6, . . . and might try to continue the sequence.

- Before the children try Questions 3 and 4 it might be necessary to discuss the meaning of 'difference'.

- In Question 3, where there is a difference of 1 at each join there will usually be a choice of matching number, for example, | 5 | 3 | 4 | 2 | or | 5 | 3 | 2 | 5 |

- In Question 4, some children might show systematically the differences when investigating the domino patterns. For example,

Difference of 1: | 6 | 5 | | 5 | 4 | | 4 | 3 | | 3 | 2 | | 2 | 1 | | 1 | 0 |

Difference of 2: | 6 | 4 | | 5 | 3 | | 4 | 2 | | 3 | 1 | | 2 | 0 |

Difference of 3: | 6 | 3 | | 5 | 2 | | 4 | 1 | | 3 | 0 |

Difference of 4 | 6 | 2 | | 5 | 1 | | 4 | 0 |

Additional activity

An extension to Question 3 could be to ask the children to make other trains with six dominoes. For example, start with a double and at each join have

a difference of 2 | 3 | 3 | | 5 | 6 | | 4 | 5 |

a difference of 3 and so on.

Discussion with the children about their approach to each problem and their findings is important.

Textbook Page 38   *Other activity: finding squares*

- This page could be tackled at any time.

- Some children might have difficulty recognising squares which are in an unusual orientation, for example, Question 1(b).

  Encourage them to rotate the page and look at each shape.

  A prepared set of overlays would be helpful to show the six squares in Question 1(c). Here are possible overlays:

   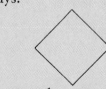

  1 square   4 squares   1 square

  For Questions 2, 3 and 4, scissors, glue and 2 cm or larger squared paper should be used to give shapes of a suitable size for handling.

Additional activity

An extension to Question 1 could be as follows:

Prepare a drawing as shown and ask the children how many squares they see.

Symmetry

Ma 1/3ab
Ma 2/3a
Ma 4/2a
Ma 4/3b
S/B1,C2
AS/B2
MD/B1
PSE
RS/A3,D2

Overview

This section

- introduces line symmetry
- provides practical work on folding shapes
- requires the completion of patterns to make them symmetrical
- provides practical work with a mirror.

	Teacher's Notes	Measure, Shape and Handling data Workbook	Textbook
Line symmetry by folding	184	30	39
Line symmetry using a mirror	185	31, 32	40
Symmetry Additional activities	187		
Problem solving			*39*
Extension		*32*	

Key words and phrases

line of symmetry   mark/draw the line of symmetry
symmetrical   make each pattern symmetrical

Resources

Useful materials

- sheets of plain paper, scissors
- paints, coloured pencils
- small (rectangular) mirrors
- squared or dotted paper
- pictures from magazines, etc.
- other materials suggested within the introductory and additional activities
- flashcards of key words and phrases

Assessment and Resources Pack

Assessment

Check-ups

Check-up 7
MSHD Workbook Pages 30–32
(Symmetry)

Resources

Problem Solving Activities
22 Jenny's necklace (2D shape patterns)
23 Shifting shapes (Symmetrical shapes)

Teaching notes

LINE SYMMETRY BY FOLDING
Introductory activities

Ma 4/3b 1/3b
S/B1

The work in this section deals with one line of symmetry only. Some suggestions for practical activities with the children are given below.

1 Folding and cutting

■ Show the children how to fold a sheet of paper and to cut through both thicknesses to make, for example, a 'skirt' shape or a simple outline of a figure:

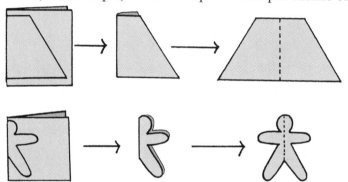

■ Discuss how on opening out the paper the two halves are identical and that the shape or figure is 'balanced'.

■ Explain that the fold line is called a 'line of symmetry' and that the shape is described as 'symmetrical'. Use flashcards to emphasise the word and phrases.

2 Folding and colouring

■ Use the 'skirt' shape to make a symmetrical pattern by applying blobs of paint to one side and folding over the shape carefully.

Ask the children to predict what will happen when the shape is unfolded. Emphasise that the *pattern* on the skirt is symmetrical. It is the *same* on either side of the fold line.

■ Use a prepared skirt shape with a coloured pattern on one side and a similar blank pattern on the other.

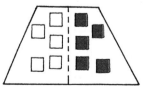

Discuss with the children the colours required in the blank squares to make the pattern symmetrical.

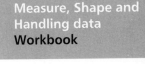
3 Folding to test for symmetry

■ Show how a shape might be folded to check for a line of symmetry.

Use some shapes (perhaps of clothes) for children to find lines of symmetry.

■ Show how a line of symmetry might be found by using a ruler placed on its edge to find a position where two halves could fold to coincide.

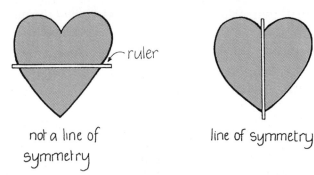

not a line of
symmetry   line of symmetry

Ma 4/3b 1/3ab
S/B1 PSE

Textbook Page 39   *Line symmetry*

A scenario of clothes is used here and on Page 30 of the Measure, Shape and Handling data Workbook. The work consolidates the introductory activities suggested above.

In Question 3, care should be taken in applying the blobs of paint – small amounts only are necessary.

Problem solving

In Question 4, the children should experiment initially by themselves. Discuss any difficulties which might arise.

Ma 4/3b 1/3b
S/B1

**Measure, Shape and
Handling data Workbook**   **Page 30**   *Line symmetry*

The clothes theme is continued here.

In Question 2, ensure that the children cut along the dotted line before they cut the shapes. Note that one item is *not* symmetrical.

LINE SYMMETRY USING A MIRROR
Introductory activities

Ma 4/3b 1/3b
S/B1,C2

The symmetry work is now extended by using a mirror

■ to find whole shapes from given half shapes

■ to assist in finding or checking a line of symmetry

■ to assist with the completion of a pattern to make it symmetrical

The following introductory activities are suggested.

1 Using a mirror

■ Show how a line of symmetry might be found using a mirror. Place the mirror on edge so that half of the symmetrical picture and its reflection in the mirror make up the whole of the *original* picture.

or

The reflected part *must* be the same as the part *behind* the mirror.

■ Repeat this activity using 2D shapes, numbers, letters, etc. Ask the children to predict the position of the line of symmetry before using the mirror to check it.

2 Completing a symmetrical pattern

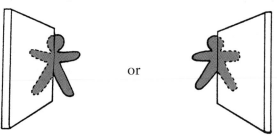

line of symmetry

■ Prepare a coloured design as shown on squared paper.

Discuss with the children which colours are required in each blank square to make the pattern symmetrical. Emphasise the position with respect to the line of symmetry of each square before it is coloured.

When the design has been completed, place a mirror along the line of symmetry both as a check and to study the reflection.

■ Repeat this activity for other designs and include horizontal and vertical lines of symmetry.

Ma 4/3b 4/2a 2/3a
S/B1 AS/B2 MD/B1 RS/A3,D2

Measure, Shape and Handling data Workbook **Textbook Page 40** *Line symmetry*

Page 40 displays half pictures, half shapes and half numerals. The children have to find the whole by placing a mirror vertically along the dotted line.

In Question 1, the outline *on the sticker* is what has to be named, while in Question 2, it is the outline *of the shape*, and not what is on it, which has to be named.

In Question3, the numerals 1, 3, 8, 0 and the signs +, −, and × are found using a mirror. Some children might require guidance to realise that answers have to be given for the calculations identified.

Ma 4/3b 1/3b
S/B1,C2

Measure, Shape and Handling data Workbook **Pages 31 and 32** *Line symmetry*

Pages 31 and 32 extend the work on line symmetry. A mirror may be used to help to find symmetry or to check symmetry.

On Page 31, Question 2, the colouring of the rectangular table mats has been kept fairly simple but some children might find it difficult.

Page 32 is difficult. It might be best to discuss Question 1 with the children before they start to colour the flags.

In Question 2, it might be best to do the first example with the children.

In Question 3, the children should make their own symmetrical patterns on sheets of squared or dotted paper and then stick these into their exercise books or on to a wall display.

Extension

SYMMETRY
Additional activities

1 Symmetry in the environment

A collection of illustrations and pictures of objects such as butterflies, insects, road signs, car badges, symbols on buildings and street markings could be gathered to provide examples of one line of symmetry.

Use these illustrations, etc., to discuss symmetry with the children.

Ask the children to look for similar examples in the environment and report their findings.

2 Sorting

Pictures cut out from magazines, etc., and some of the above, could be used for a group activity.

Ask the children in a group to discuss which pictures show line symmetry and which do not. The pictures could then be displayed in two sets headed 'symmetrical' and 'not symmetrical'.

Ma 1/3b
Ma 2/3e
Ma 3/3a
Ma 4/2a
Ma 5/2a
Ma 5/3abc
C/A2,B1,2
O/C2,B1,A2
D/C2
I/B1
T/B3
PS/B2,3
PSE

Handling data

Overview

This section

- introduces decision diagrams

- provides opportunities for and practice in collecting, organising, displaying and interpreting data

- introduces the use of a scaled axis on bar graphs

- introduces the terms 'very unlikely', 'unlikely' and 'likely', 'very likely'.

	Teacher's Notes	Measure, Shape and Handling data Workbook	Textbook
Decision diagrams	190	33, 34	
Bar graphs: scaled axis	193	35–38	41, 42
Extracting information			43
Probability: likelihood	196		44
Other activities			*45*
Investigation		*37, 38*	
Extension			*43*
Problem solving			*45*

Key words and phrases

graph	sentence	very likely
tick sheet	minute	likely
most often	half past	unlikely
least often	quarter past	very unlikely

Resources

Useful materials

- scissors

- coloured pencils or crayons

- packet of sweets

- 1 cm or 2 cm squared paper

- bouncing ball, bench

- other materials suggested within the introductory activities

- flashcards of key words and phrases

Assessment and Resources Pack

Assessment

Check-ups

Check-up 8
MSHD Workbook Pages 33–38
(Handling data)

Resources

Problem Solving Activities

24 Pets (Graph interpretation)
25 How likely (Probability activity)

Resource Cards

Resource Cards 22 to *24* (Clothes show) can be used for handling data activities.

Teaching notes

DECISION DIAGRAMS
Introductory activities

Ma 5/2a 1/3b
C/B1 I/B1

Decision diagrams form the first part of the work in the Handling data section which is set in the context of a visit to a Leisure Complex. The complex contains a Leisure Centre, a Cinema, a Bowling Alley and a Café.

1 Leisure Complex

Pictures of people participating in a range of recreational activities could be used to promote a discussion on a Leisure Complex. Ask the children

'Has anyone visited a Leisure Complex?'

'What sort of things did you see or do there?'

and so on.

2 Signs in the Complex

■ Discuss with the children how they might find their way around an unfamiliar place. Suggest the idea of using signs. Make a list or display of signs with which the children might be familiar. For example,

■ Ask 'What kind of signs might be found at a Leisure Complex?' These could be drawn and displayed. For example,

 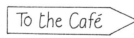

■ Ask the children to sort a collection of prepared signs according to the following criteria:

Signs giving information

Signs telling us to do something

Signs telling us *not* to do something

Signs giving direction

The last two types of sign are especially important for the work on decision diagrams.

3 Following signs

This activity should be carried out with a group of children. It gives practice in following signs and making decisions.

■ Make four pairs of decision cards as shown

■ Draw this plan on a large sheet of paper and place the decision cards at each junction as shown.

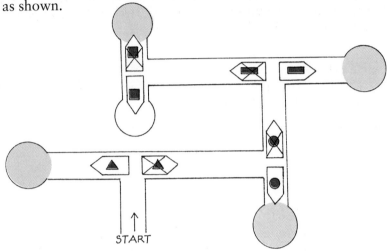

■ Make six pairs of shape cards as shown, (or use plastic shapes).

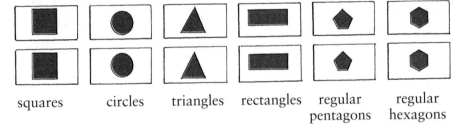

squares   circles   triangles   rectangles   regular   regular
                                                  pentagons hexagons

■ Place the shape cards in a pile at the START.

Each child in turn, picks a shape card, moves to the first junction showing two decision cards and makes a decision as to which way to move. For example,

If the child's shape card has a triangle the card is moved in this direction.   If the child's shape card does *not* have a triangle the card is moved in this direction.

■ The child moves his/her shape card to the next junction where another decision has to be made and so on.

When all the shapes have been sorted one shaded area should contain circles, another squares, another rectangles and the other pentagons and hexagons.

■ Ask the children to investigate what happens when the decision cards are placed at different junctions.

191

Pages 33 and 34 provide a 'decision' board for each child. The purpose of the activity is that each card showing a picture of a child or group of children on Page 34 has to be moved to a particular part of the Leisure Complex by following paths and making decisions based on the pair of signs at each junction.

■ The child should cut out the pictures on Page 34. A picture shows either a single named child or a group of children, one of whom is named. Each named child carries two items which are coloured.

The items are   a bag – blue or red
                a bowl – green or red
                a ticket – yellow or green
                an ice cream cone – yellow or blue

■ The pictures should be placed in a pile at the START. The child takes one picture at a time, looks at it and also at the first pair of signs. A decision has to be made at each pair of signs.

For example,

A picture showing a child carrying a blue bag should be moved in this direction to a part of the Leisure Complex.

A picture showing a child *not* carrying a blue bag, i.e. a differently coloured bag or no bag at all, should be moved in this direction along a path to the next pair of signs, where another decision has to be taken.

■ The activity ends when all the pictures have been placed in the four parts of the Leisure Complex.

■ It would be helpful to 'talk through' the movement of the first picture with the children. For example, Kapil,

'Is Kapil in a group or on his own?'   (*Group*)
'Which way should he go?'
Kapil moves to the next pair of signs.

'Does Kapil have a blue bag?'   (*No*)
'Which way should he go?'
Kapil moves to the next pair of signs.

'Does Kapil have a green ticket?'   (*Yes*)
Place Kapil's card in the Cinema.

■ Ask the children to try an example on their own, and check to see if the picture has been placed in the correct location.

■ On completion of the activity, questions could be asked such as 'Who is at the Leisure Centre?' and so on.

BAR GRAPHS: SCALED AXIS
Introductory activities

In Heinemann Mathematics 2, the children were introduced to horizontal and vertical bar graphs where one square represented one unit. They also used tick sheets to collect and organise data. The work is now extended to include bar graphs where one square represents two units.

Ma 5/3b
C/A2,B2 O/A2 D/C2

The context of the Leisure Complex is continued and provides work related to Litter, Sam's Café, the Leisure Centre and the Cinema.

1 Litter in the playground

Measure, Shape and Handling data Workbook, Pages 35 and 36 deal with litter at the Leisure Complex. Discuss with the children the problem of litter around their own school. Ask each child to collect two or three pieces of litter from the playground. Once collected the litter could be sorted into two, three or more sets using sheets of paper for each category, for example,

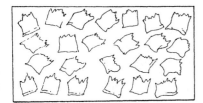
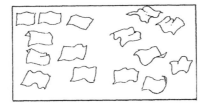
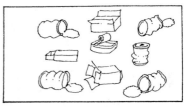

crisp bags	24

sweet wrappers	15

cartons/cans	9

2 Introducing a bar graph with a simple scale

The above information should be represented as a horizontal or vertical bar graph with a one-to-one scale.

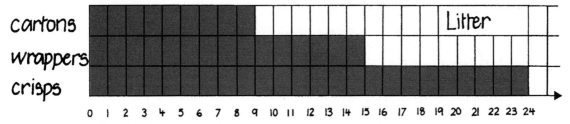

Show the children that the same data could be represented as a horizontal bar graph where one square represents 2 units.

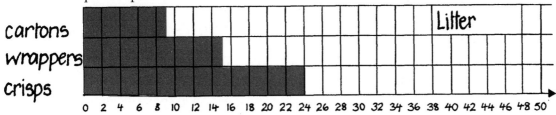

When marking the bar for the sweet wrappers (15) emphasise that '15' is half-way between 14 and 16. Similarly, the bar for the cartons is half-way between 8 and 10.

193

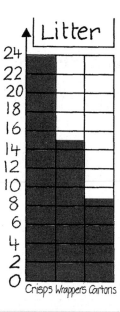

The above work could be repeated to introduce simple scale on a vertical bar graph.

Ma 5/2a 5/3b 1/3b
C/B1 O/B1,C2 D/C2 I/B1

Measure, Shape and Handling data Workbook **Pages 35 and 36** *Handling data: introducing a scaled axis*

The children should look at each part of the Leisure Complex. They should count, by ticking if necessary, each litter item and record it in the table. All the answers are even to make the drawing of the graph easier.

On Page 36, Question 5, the children should refer back to the map on Measure, Shape and Handling data Workbook, Pages 33 and 34, to decide where to place the litter bin. There is no correct answer. What is important is the discussion involved.

Ma 5/2a 5/3b
C/B1,2 O/B1 D/C2 I/B1

Investigation

Measure, Shape and Handling data Workbook **Pages 37 and 38** *Handling data*

Pages 37 and 38 give further practice in completing a tick sheet (introduced in Heinemann Mathematics 2) and in drawing a horizontal and a vertical bar graph, both with a scaled axis, using the context of Sam's Café.

The collection of data on Page 37, Question 1, could be organised as follows. Each child chooses a flavour from those given and writes it on a separate piece of paper. These pieces of paper are collected and put in a box. Each group of children then uses the data in the box to complete the tick sheet. Ensure that the children write the totals in the column at the right of the tick sheet. The bar graph should then be completed.

On Page 38, the children should score out each sweet as it is counted and put a tick in the tick sheet. Once the graph is drawn it would be worthwhile discussing with the children if they agree with the statement at the top of the page.

Investigation

The investigation in Question 3 gives the children an opportunity to collect, organise, display and interpret information. The sweets could be sorted by size, or shape, or colour, or texture, etc. The method of finding how many in each set and the way in which to record this information should be left open-ended. It is not necessary for children to display this information graphically, though some may choose to do so, in which case they will certainly need to be shown how to draw, label and number the axes as appropriate.

Textbook Pages 41 and 42   *Handling data*

On both Pages 41 and 42, a graph with a scaled axis is presented for
interpretation. The children have to collect, organise and display information
for a similar theme. The work is set within the context of the Leisure Centre.

On Page 41, Questions 1 and 2, the children should use the scale on the
vertical axis to read values from the graph. The absence of horizontal lines
running through the graph is designed to encourage this skill.

In Question 3, the required data could be collected using the method suggested
on Page 000 of the Teacher's Notes for Measure, Shape and Handling data
Workbook, Page 37, Question 1. Even though a tick sheet format is outlined
on Textbook Page 41, the children will probably need help in making one of
their own. They will certainly need help to draw a graph of their results. Show
them how

- to draw the two axes
- to write the scale on one axis
- to label the axes
- to give the graph a title

Discuss the completed graph with the children so that they have some ideas for
Question 3(c).

Page 42 involves the children in timing activities for one minute. Such work is
introduced in the Time section in the Measure, Shape and Handling data
Workbook and it is advisable that this work is completed before children try
Textbook Page 42.

In Question 1, the children should use the scale on the *horizontal* axis to read
values from the graph. In Question 1(d) the children should be encouraged to
find the 'difference between' from the graph.

In Question 2 each group member should have the opportunity

- to time a minute
- to record the scores

The children should be encouraged to draw a graph similar to the one at the
top of Textbook Page 42, but might require assistance to do this correctly.

Textbook Page 43   *Handling data: extracting information*

Before the children attempt Page 43 they should have completed the work on
Time in the Measure, Shape and Handling data Workbook. Page 43 gives the
children the opportunity to interpret data in a non-graphical format.

Question 4 is challenging as it asks the children to find films for a day of the
week which is *not* written on the display, i.e. Thursday.

Question 5 is similar to Question 4. This time the children are asked to find a
film that will still be showing at 9.30, though this time does not appear on the
display.

Ma 5/3c 1/3b

The terms 'impossible', 'uncertain' and 'certain' were introduced in Heinemann Mathematics 2. The language of 'very unlikely', 'unlikely', 'likely' and 'very likely' is now introduced to describe certain events and situations.

1 Very unlikely, very likely

Discuss events and situations within the experience of the children and decide whether they are best described using the terms 'very unlikely' or 'very likely'. Such discussion could involve statements like the following to which children respond by saying 'very unlikely' or 'very likely':

I will use a pencil today.
Prince Charles will visit our school today.
I will grow 20 cm this year.
I will eat something today.
Our teacher will give each of us a bar of chocolate.
I will have my hair cut this year.

The two terms 'very unlikely' and 'very likely' could be presented on a line as shown.

2 Unlikely, likely

Discuss events and situations where the terms 'unlikely' and 'likely' might be used, for example,

I will see a bus today.
The teacher will read us a story today.
I will have homework tonight.
I will sharpen my pencil today.
It will snow this week.
I will be given a present this week.

Some of these statements may elicit different responses depending on the circumstance.

The two terms 'likely' and 'unlikely' could be added to the line.

3 Very unlikely, unlikely, likely, very likely

Ask the children to make up their own statements. Discuss with them the term that best describes the event. After sufficient practice in using the above terms, the examples which follow on Textbook Page 44 could be considered.

Textbook Page 44 *Handling data: likelihood*

There are no 'correct' answers to the statements in Questions 1 to 6. For
example, in certain schools the best term to describe Statement 1 may be 'very
likely' while in other schools where there has been an anti-litter campaign, the
most appropriate term may be 'unlikely'.

The discussion which arises from each statement is as important as the answer.

Textbook Page 45 *Other activity: patterns and sequences*

■ This page could be attempted at any time. The activities on Page 45 require the
children to identify, extend and devise patterns and sequences involving
number, shape and colour.

■ In Questions 1(a)(b) and (c), the children need to consider only one attribute.
For the remaining questions in which two attributes are considered, the
children should be encouraged to identify and then continue one attribute
pattern, say shape, before identifying and continuing the second attribute
pattern, say colour.

Index